Hilda Austi Linder

SMALL MOCCASIN TRACKS:

Memories of an Alaskan Mountain Family

HILDA LUSTER-LINDNER

SUTTON, ALASKA

Relevant Publishers LLC
P.O. Box 505
Sutton, AK 99674

Visit our website at www.relevantpublishers.com

Printed in the United States of America

Luster-Lindner, Hilda
Small Moccasin Tracks: Memories of an Alaskan Mountain
Family / Hilda Luster-Lindner – 2nd ed.

ISBN: 978-0-99926-052-4 (paperback)
      978-0-99926-053-1 (ebook)

LCCN: 2018948473

DEDICATION:

For my mother.
She was a tiny woman with a lot of strength.
She gave us everything she could to grow up
strong, and it was more than enough.

Mother holding Stella.
On the horse (front to rear): Lucy, Bonnie, and Fay

CHAPTER 1

The frost made pretty ferns on the window glass. The children blew on the ice with their warm breath to make a peephole. They wanted to watch the snow falling on that cold day in January 1950. Earlier that fall, their mother had the children chink the cracks in the log cabin walls with moss and old rags to keep out the cold and wind. Now they couldn't look through the cracks as they had in the summer. This was a much better cabin than most of the places they had lived. There was a real tarpaper roof and one of the windows even had glass. There was also a real stove for cooking and warming the cabin, although it was not warming the cabin on that day since it had no fire in it.

Small Moccasin Tracks

Their mother was still in bed, something was not right, as she was always up before anyone. She always had a fire in the stove and a full teakettle heating to wash little hands and faces, as well as maybe a cup of tea. Breakfast was always ready before most of the children were even awake and out of their beds. The oldest child, Lucy, was always a big help to her mother with the younger children. She would help by dressing her smaller sisters, adding coats and blankets to keep them warm and put them on the bunk by the glass window. Then gave them each a piece of frozen moose meat to chew on.

Their mother was not ill; she was in labor with her latest child. As she had with all the others before, she delivered the baby and cut the cord herself, trying not to cry out too much and frighten her other children. I was a large, robust and loud baby, and I have remained so, even through adulthood, to this very day. Just two years earlier mother had given birth to twins in a small trappers cabin at the head of the Boulder Creek. They were small and premature, a boy and a girl. The boy was too small and didn't live but a few minutes. He was buried under the cache house of a pine tree so the animals wouldn't get him. The girl though tiny was a scrappy little thing. She was so small in fact, that one of father's hunters gave mother a shoebox to keep her in. They had two boxes, but one was used to bury the boy. They named the daughter, Stella, and were able to use the shoebox as a crib for a month before she out grew it. She is still a scrapper even to this day.

After birthing her twins on that morning on Boulder Creek, mother had to get up and cook breakfast for father's hunting party. The other children needed to be fed and taken care of as well. Mother stayed in the main camp for a month, cooking and running the base camp. The older children helped mother to care for little Stella, since there was a lot to do in running a base camp. Food had to be prepared for everyone for three meals a day. Bread had to be made from scratch, since there was no store nearby to buy it from in those days. Lunches had to be packed for any of the hunters that would be out. Camp must be kept clean; clothes were washed on a washboard and hung out on lines to dry, and the horses needed to be looked after. Any horses with sores or lameness were treated. Mother would put lard on the saddle sores so they would heal, and it helped keep the bugs off.

The older girls found a way to keep little Stella from crying, that is until mother caught them. They put Stella in a flour sack and dipped her in the ice-cold creek until she would stop crying. I guess she was quite loud for such a small baby. Luckily, she was tough, as I don't know how Stella didn't drown or chill to death in that creek. Mother spanked them both and tied Stella in a cloth around her chest while she worked for a while. I would see tears sometimes as mother worked.

Mother was a tiny woman, only four foot nine inches tall and maybe a hundred pounds soaking wet. She was a strong woman in body and mind. She had to be. Mother had fifteen pregnancies and raised eight children, mostly by herself as father was away much of the time guiding hunting trips and trapping. Mother had to drag large logs on her back. Then she'd chop them up for our fires so she could cook our food and keep us warm. There were no warm gloves or winter clothes for mother to wear, only a few army surplus left over from WW2. Her hands and feet would crack and bleed with the cold and hard work, but she had to keep going for all of us children. I never heard mother complained, although I saw tears many times. Sometimes I would hear her crying after she thought we were all asleep. What a heart she had to keep going all those years for her children.

Mother had a wonderful garden each summer no matter where we lived. She grew many magnificent things in her gardens, with always a few flowers to feed the eyes. I loved our garden. Many times I had my backside warmed when mother caught me sneaking to eat new peas and carrots, but they were so darn good. Fresh from the earth, I can still remember their taste today. They were so very good! Only as an adult I learned the importance of mother's garden.

In the fall mother would have all the children help dig a large hole in a nearby hillside. She would make layers of alternating vegetables and hay. Then she would cover the layers with a couple feet of earth. Potatoes, carrots and cabbage were kept fresh over the winter that way. Other vegetables were either canned or dried. Even stew was canned for winter stores. When it would get cold enough and snow came, any meat would go under the snow. Moose, caribou, and sometimes Dall sheep all were put in our outdoor snow freezer. The snow was kept the meat fresh just like an electric freezer, except the meat was not cut up or packaged. We just chopped off a chunk of frozen meat when it was needed with an ax.

I really don't know how mother did it, but she hand sewed our clothes and washed them on a washboard. Working out side in the snow, sun, or rain, she provided basic food and shelter for all of us kids. How she fed us was amazing in itself. We ate a lot of moose and caribou, and beaver tail with beans was always a treat. Everyone loved moose tongue, and marrow bones boiled with vegetables was also really great. The older girls, Lucy and Fay, hunted small game with an old 4.10 and .22 over and under gun. They learned to be pretty good shots, so as not to waste bullets. Therefore the cooking pot was graced with many squirrels, rabbits, spruce grouse and ptarmigan.

God blessed us with many lakes, rivers, and streams too. All were teaming with many kinds of fish. There were a few winters when fish was all the meat we had to eat. One winter we ate so many salmon that I can hardly look a salmon in the eye today. A few times when game could not be found, we had to eat what was available from our livestock. Occasionally, we ate horses, and once we had a mule. Well let's just say mother made sure we were fed to the best of her abilities.

Of course when father was home we had plenty of meat. He always left meat under the snow; it just ran out sometimes before winter ended. It wasn't just children that needed to be fed. We had dogs to feed, sometimes a lot of dogs. We had fifty to one hundred dogs at times. We needed those dogs. They were very important as winter transportation and summer packing. Father used them on the trap line and freighting supplies too.

My father, John Luster, was a well-known trapper and hunting guide in Alaska. Many stories have been written about him, both in books and hunting magazines, of course not all the stories were true. He was a trapper and guide first in Wyoming; then in 1946, he moved his family to Alaska. The reason for the move he claimed was that Wyoming was getting too populated. I think it may have had more to do with to many ex-wives, and the sheriffs frowning on his hunting and trapping activities. In any case, father was busy with his outdoorsman life style and wasn't around home much. He'd check in periodically, mostly to see the new babies, and start another baby that mother would deliver alone with only the children to help her. When I was young, I could never remember what he looked liked. If father came home with someone, I always waited to see which man the other children ran toward. I had made the mistake before of greeting the wrong man as father and didn't want to repeat it. I was as happy to see him as the other children; I just didn't know it was him when he returned.

Those first couple of years after the family had moved to Alaska, home was a cabin in the nearly abandoned coal town of Chickaloon. I say nearly abandoned, as its only inhabitants were a few families of Athabascan heritage. There had once been a thriving town in Chickaloon; now most of the homes were gone and only a few cabins remained. Here and there a fire hydrant could be seen standing in a field or by a path. There were many foundations left scattered through the woods and fields. On a hill were piles of bricks where once a lavish home had stood. Many of those bricks eventually made their way to flower bed boarders. There were two railroad bridges that had been converted to car and horse bridges. Big thick planks had been nailed down to the trestle in two rows just wide enough to fit the cars and truck wheels. We rode horses across as well. A few horses had fallen off into the river through the trusses and had to swim out. Stella fell through once when she was about six years old. Thankfully she caught on a beam under the trestle and was saved from drowning. Lucy and Fay dragged her back up with a rope.

Another time, a horse fell off the planks but didn't fall all the way to the river. His legs were wedged tight between the beams. Father got a saw and cut him out. The horse came out fine, but I don't think that helped the bridge much. In those days, people would come to places like Chickaloon to experience the native lifestyle. Taking pictures of native people with dog teams and salmon wheels and such things as native people did in their daily life. My mother was unfamiliar with this practice. When a group of city ladies came to ask her for pictures, she obliged them but had them wait a few minutes while she got dressed for their pictures. Mother went in the cabin and quickly put on her one good dress and pinned her hair up. Those ladies took some pictures of mother and some of the children with a dog team. But they wanted pictures of mother dressed in a parka or some type of native dress. One of the native ladies that lived in a cabin nearby told mother that if she dressed in a fashion that pleased those city ladies, they would give her a few dollars. Mother never made that mistake again. If city people wanted wild Indian pictures, that is what they got from then on. I don't think those city people thought of us as being human. They thought of us as part of an interesting picture they could talk about seeing when they went back to the lower forty-eight states.

We spent a lot of time in the children's homes in those days. There were territorial nurses that went around to the native families in the bush. Apparently, natives were incapable of caring for their children, or so it seemed to white city folks. You know we were all a bunch of heathens. What did the native people do for ten thousand years before the white man came to civilize us and save our souls? Therefore the nurses came, and when they saw some thing they didn't understand or didn't like, off we went to the children's homes. They always brought us back home after a while though. I guess we were a lot of trouble or maybe not house broken. I went to the children's home shortly after I was born. Mother had no milk to breast feed me. She tried to feed me carnation canned milk, but I seemed not to thrive. Mother had much to do and not enough time to hold me with a bottle. She would prop a bottle in my mouth and go on about her work. Father came home and figured out right away what was wrong. He had mother give me a bottle as she always did. He hid behind the door and watched. My two year old sister, Stella, crept in looking all around, then she grabbed the bottle sucked it down, popped it back in my mouth and ran. Ah, the puzzle was solved. In her defense Stella was hungry. She couldn't get enough food down at a time, and she had rickets. So, off to the children's home we both went. Of course I don't remember that time. I don't think I came back home until my mother had another child, my little brother Johnny. I am not sure, as I was a baby and can only go by what I have been told.

One of the first things I do remember was when I almost drowned. There was a small creek in the meadow in front of our house. It was only a yard wide in spots. The two oldest girls (Lucy and Fay) had laid small poles over the creek in a narrow place so they could run over the creek without getting their feet wet. The big girls wanted to play by themselves and tried to get away from the little kids. When I was quite young, maybe two and a half years old, I tried to follow them. The girls tried to chase me back, but I have always been stubborn and followed anyway. They tried to get away from me by running over the poles and hiding on the other side. I ran after them on my short little legs, but

I was far behind. When I came to the creek, it never occurred to me to try to cross on the poles. I just ran straight into the creek. Even though the creek was only a yard wide, it was also over a yard deep. I can still remember the feeling of the grass pulling loose from the mud on the bank of the creek as I tried to cling to it. Lucky for me, those big girls had only stopped to hide in the bushes on the other side of the creek. They were watching to see if I had gone home. When they saw what had happened, they came running back to pull me out before I drowned. They took me back to the house where mother warmed my backside for going near the creek. I think I was already cured of the desire to go near that creek for quite some time, long before I reached mother or the house.

Now at least the big girls could truly get away from me. I guess my near drowning turned out okay for everyone. When I was a little older and in the winter, mother went thirty-two miles to the nearest town to get supplies. We were told to stay in the doghouse to stay safe and warm until she returned. The dog had puppies, so really there was milk if we needed it. Don't you know along comes a traveling territorial nurse while mother was gone? Off we went again to the children's home. I am sure the nurse must have left some kind of note so mother would know where we were; otherwise, mother would have been worried.

The nurses also came by to give shots and vitamins. All the children hated the shots, but none as much as Stella. She found a way to beat the nurses. Stella would hide in a doghouse at the first sign of a nurse. The nurse would not get too close to the doghouse, as the dog would bite. Usually the nurse had to wait until Stella was in a children's home before she could give her shots. Even then, it took two extra staff to hold Stella down for those shots. The nurses should have forgotten the dog; Stella was more dangerous. She would bite and draw blood with her teeth at any body part that got close enough to touch her. The children's homes were segregated by ages. School age children went one place, and little children went to another. We would not see our siblings for months at a time. But we did see a doctor during those visits, so I guess there was some good to come out of it. My brother Johnny and I became inseparable during those times. Both being little, we were grouped together and were all the family we had for months on end. It sometimes seemed like forever in those children's homes. Johnny and I are still very close and will remain so forever I think.

When Johnny and I were three and four years old, we were at a children's home near the town of Palmer. It was a small dairy farm and had about fifty milk cows. There was a large barn with a hayloft. Behind the barn was a large manure pit. We, the little guys, could walk on it as the top had a slight crust on it. Underneath the crust, it was actually about six feet deep with liquid manure. We were told to stay away from the pit, as it was a danger. The folks that ran the children's home had a son of about twelve years old. He took Johnny and I up to the loft and had us hold onto an open umbrella. He told us if we jumped out of the loft and held on tight we would float down to the ground. Of course, it sounded like great fun. We held on tight and jumped out the loft door. The boy's father walked around the corner just in time to see us crash right through the manure pit's crust and deep into the pile. He jumped in and pulled us out, saving our lives. On top of getting his backside warmed with a belt, that boy had to clean us up. I think cleaning Johnny and me was probably worse punishment than the spanking. The boy was pretty mad at us for crashing into the pit. He scrubbed us pretty hard with the brush and sprayed us with the hose from the cow lot to rinse us off. We were some scratched up and raw-skinned children. Johnny and I never believed anything that boy told us ever again. Father liked to tease us with stories he would make up about Johnny and me. They were very sad stories for small children. One he told me went like this:

> Poor little Hilda was lost way out in the woods. She had lost her coat and hat. Then she fell into a deep, icy-cold hole. Moose and wolves were running around the top of the hole. She couldn't get out, because they would eat her. Poor little Hilda was hungry and freezing. She cried and called for someone to help her, but no one heard her, and that was because they were all at home sitting by the warm fire eating ice cream and pie.

At that point, I would start to howl. Father would laugh, as did everyone the story didn't happen to be about. Sometimes father would rough house with Johnny and I. One or both of us always wound up crying. He would have Johnny and I wrestle. I was pretty tough and a little bigger than Johnny, so most of the time I came out on top. One time that changed. We were wrestling near the big twenty-gallon water cans, and I flipped back and knocked myself out. I guess Johnny was the winner that day.

Father played kind of rough at times. Maybe he thought we were stronger than we were. He left bite marks on our arms and legs. They were just marks, no broken skin. Sometimes our legs and arms hurt when held them behind our backs, and we would cry. Whenever we cried, father would get angry with us and ask if we were sissies. He would ask little Johnny if he was a man or a mouse. I guess father just wanted us to be tough. We did get tough and strong and self-reliant too, which was what father really wanted. Father seemed to spend extra time with Johnny and I when he was home. I think because Johnny was the only son that he got to raise himself. Father had to put up with me as a sidekick since Johnny and I were always together. Father was happy that he had a boy in the house. After all, the rest of the children in our family were girls.

We did have other half brothers and sisters, but they lived in other states. We never knew any of them until we were much older. Our brother, John Joseph, came to Alaska when we were teenagers. Our brother Michael died in a plane crash before I was born. I also met two other sisters in California years later. They both had children my age. They were city women, while we were all rough around the edges. We never got to know our half siblings well. Nor did we spend much time with them, as our lives were so different. I think most of them live in Arizona now.

A most awful thing happened to me when I was four years old. I barely remember some of it, which is probably a blessing. Johnny and I were being brought home from another extended stay at the children's home courtesy of our visiting territorial nurse. Someone drove us back to a ranch at the trailhead where we would meet up with father, mother, and the other children. We could then be brought back to our beautiful valley by horseback. One child would be put in each side pannier, and a larger child would ride on a padded packsaddle with a foot in each pannier to keep them level. Mother liked to stop at that ranch whenever she had the chance to visit the wife of the rancher. Mother didn't get to see other women very often; so, it was a happy occasion for her. There were also some children of the same age as two of my older sisters. All the children liked to play in and around the lake that was only a few yards from the rancher's doorstep. They had a dock and a boat. We were not allowed to play in the boat, but playing on the dock was okay. We could also play around the shallow at the water's edge.

Mother with kids in panniers

I had on a nice clean outfit. A little skirt and blouse with shoes and socks. I also had ribbons on my braids. The staff always dressed us nice to go home. It was an hour ride from the children's home to the trailhead with no potty break. Now, I needed to go. Mother had Lucy take me to the outhouse. Lucy set me on the seat and instantly forgot about me. She just turned around and continued her visit with the ranch kids. Lucy was hanging out the door as far as she could because it was summer and the outhouse was full. I remember sitting on the edge of a huge hole, holding onto the edge of the seat as tightly as I could teetering forward and back. Then I lost my grip. I fell over backward in a swan dive into the hole. Father fished me out with a rake someone handed him. Then he carried me on the end of the rake down to the lake, which luckily was only a few yards away. He dunked me in the lake and swished me around with the rake, getting off the worst of it. Sadly, he cut my clothes off with his pocketknife and both my braids. I screamed as my beautiful ribbons floated away still attached to my braids. Father told me to shut up, and he would buy me new ribbons. I never got new ribbons. Of course I didn't need them till my hair grew out anyway. What I remember is that none of the other children would sit by me or play with me for quite a while after I fell in that outhouse hole. Thank God I don't remember the time I spent swimming down below.

Mother was an advocate of self-medication. Her most commonly used home remedies were kerosene and turpentine. It was used for everything including but not limited to colds and flu, cuts and scrapes, and internal problems. Therefore when three of my older sisters were busy playing with axe heads, throwing them in the air to see who could get theirs highest, there was an accident. One of the ax heads came down to graze the top of Lucy's head like a Mohawk. Yes, mother pulled the ax head out of the top of Lucy's head and poured in the turpentine. I don't think Lucy has been the same since. When Bonnie jumped on a pitchfork, running it through her foot, mother pulled out the pitchfork, and you guessed it, poured on the turpentine. Which brings me to my chance at the turpentine.

We rarely wore shoes, as we rarely had any money for shoes. Our feet were quite tough, but sadly no match for a broken bottle I found. I was running and my foot landed on a broken bottle half buried in the dirt. My foot was cut to the bone from one side to the other on the bottom. Mother rinsed my foot with water then poured on turpentine. The flesh on my foot turned white. Mother tied a rag around my foot and sent me on my way. Well, the turpentine deadened the nerves so I didn't feel much pain after awhile.

The turpentine didn't seem to work well in healing my foot. It began to smell rather bad and turned black for quite a ways around the cut. It so happened that a soldier from one of the military bases in Anchorage was camping at the lake nearby. We went there to beg candy as the military always had C-rations. He saw me limping along and was horrified when he looked at my foot. He went to my mother and told her I needed to see a doctor.

Mother refused his offer to take me to the hospital. He then talked her into letting him treat my foot. She agreed as long as I stayed in the valley. That soldier drove his beat up old car the thirty-two miles to Palmer, the nearest town, and bought medical supplies. When he came back, he cleaned my foot with some kind of antiseptic wash and cut off all the dead and rotting flesh. He put something on that stung like crazy and bandaged it up with gauze and tape. He then put a large white sock on my foot that went all the way to my belt loop, which is where he tied it. I stayed in his tent on a blanket for a week. After that, I went home, but he came by for another week. Every day he changed the bandage and checked my progress. Thanks to him, I have a foot in good working order today.

Father bought a large grazing lease that was located on the tidal flats of the Cook Inlet, which is where we kept the horses in the winter. Where the horses went, so did we. There was plenty of sea grass for the horses, but not much of a house for us to live in. The tide flats have a great amount of migratory birds in spring and fall, which draws waterfowl hunters there. Many of the local hunters built small shacks to stay in while they hunted ducks and geese.

Most of the shacks were just eight by ten feet long, but some men had acquired the old jail when they moved the town of Old Matanuska to higher ground. The town was renamed Palmer. The old jail was a ten by twelve foot building and relocated near the mouth of the Matanuska River slough. They pulled the building on a sled down the slough in the winter on the ice. Father built shelves across the back of the shack, which became our beds. The children slept two to a shelf, end to end. The little guys slept on the bottom for two reasons. First, they didn't have far to fall. The second and most important reason was so they wouldn't baptize anyone under them when they slept, as they weren't very house broke.

The cabin was small and not hard to heat, which was good as there wasn't much wood out there on the flats. Wood had to be dragged in with a workhorse or dog team from a mile or more away. And we had to wait for the mud to freeze in the fall in order to get it. The mud in Cook Inlet is very dangerous. It will grip the legs of man or animal alike and pull you in. If they can't pull free, they will die at the next incoming tide. Many people over the years have died this way.

There were two men that got caught in the mud while duck hunting. One got out, but the other didn't. The man that got free tried to help the other out, and when that failed he had the man that was stuck try to breath through an empty shot gun barrel. It didn't work for long, and the man eventually drowned. Even after the tide went back out, they had a hard time retrieving the body. They finally pulled him out with a helicopter. I never saw that, but I read about it in the newspaper later. We were told to always stay away from the slough and the telling was reinforced with a willow switch if we were caught near the mud.

We mostly listened to what mother told us when we were small. After all, she was the authority figure and pretty much the sole adult in our lives most of the time. Father wasn't given to spanking us when he was home. We had to do something really awful to get him to correct us at all, and then it was usually only for safety measures or if we were doing something that would affect the livestock adversely. Other than that, it was mother that molded our early years.

Mother with Lucy and Bonnie

CHAPTER 2

In the summer of 1954 father bought a truckload of donkeys out of Mexico. They were trucked from Mexico to Alaska. It was a long trip and took quite a while, as when they got to the Al-Can highway, it was all gravel and rough with potholes and washouts. It was pretty rough going with bridges washing out and the road washing away in spots too. People were sometimes stuck right in the middle of the road in mud. They had to wait for help to be pulled out. Sometimes people were stranded for days while work was done to fix the road for travel. There were 1600 miles of the Al-Can highway in rough condition back then. My brother,

Johnny, and I were waiting with great excitement and had many plans for those donkeys. Father had promised we could have one of those donkeys to ride. What on earth was he thinking? They weren't tame donkeys; they were wild donkeys. Unfortunately, we didn't know that.

The donkey truck arrived during the night while we were sleeping. We didn't know about them until morning when we got up. When we woke, father told Johnny and I that our donkeys were there. The donkeys had been turned loose in the big horse pasture to rest up after their hard trip north. Father told Johnny and I that if we could catch one of those donkeys, we could have it. We grabbed a halter and headed out to catch us a donkey.

Father was sure we would never catch one, but he watched us from where he was drinking coffee with the truckers. We just got into the field when a large donkey trotted off the hillside. Johnny and I ran after it with our ropes in hand. This was a nice big, brown donkey; just perfect, if we could just catch it. We were in hot pursuit when father looked up to check our progress. Well, what he saw took him by surprise and woke him up in a hurry. He ran into the house and grabbed his gun. Then he loaded it as he ran. He shot that grizzly bear we were chasing just before we caught up to it. Well, we had never seen a donkey before. We what we were chasing didn't look like a horse or cow. It was also large enough for both Johnny and I to ride. We figured it was a perfect donkey, until father shot it. In the end, the good news was mother had plenty of lard to bake pies and bread. We also ate bear steak for breakfast. Father made sausage, and we had meat for a while too. Father gave the bear hide to the truckers, and they reduced the price of hauling the donkeys in exchange.

It worked out well for everyone. Later that day, Johnny and I found out what a donkey really looked like.

We had a lot of fun with the donkeys. Later, the big girls broke them to ride and pull. Lucy and Fay would hook up a couple donkeys to the hay wagon and take us for rides all over the countryside. Bridget and Jenny were the best donkeys for pulling. A large gelded Jack named Oscar turned out to be best for riding. Most of the other donkeys were used for packing or were sold to other people. Those donkeys learned how to keep us off their backs. When we tried to climb on, they would put their heads down, and with no withers, we would just slide down their necks. Sometimes when we finally managed to get on one, they would be walking along and stop suddenly. As they stopped, they would put their necks down and off we would slide. It was really great fun. I think donkey and children all enjoyed the game.

In the winter of 1954, our little two-room house burned down. I am taking some liberty calling it a house. Father built it, and he was by no means a carpenter. It would have looked more like a corn crib if not for the tar paper nailed all over it. It really didn't need windows, because you could see anything happening outside by simply looking through the cracks in the walls. There were cracks in the floorboards so large the silverware would fall through. When we had nothing left to eat with, one of the smaller children would crawl under the floorboards and hand everything they found back up through the cracks. While it wasn't good by most people's standards, it was our real good house. Most of the time, we lived in tents or under a large spruce tree with lots of limbs built out like a wicki-up. You can imagine how up set mother must have been to lose her only real house. It was a real hard blow for her. Father had just come back from one of his trap lines and had spent the last couple of days putting his furs on stretchers to dry, half a winter's work.

Thankfully, all the children got out safely, but not much else made it. Father grabbed two bags of what he thought was laundry stacked by the door. Mother grabbed a little child in each arm and two blankets. Lucy and Fay both grabbed a couple of coats. Fay also got her little flat-faced doll father had carved for her from a board. Then Lucy and Fay herded Stella and Bonnie out the door. Stella and Bonnie got out wearing just their shirts. The two little children were Johnny and I. Mother laid out a blanket on the snow. Putting all the children in the middle, she opened the duffel bags father had pulled from the fire and found he had grabbed two bags of wool socks that had come from the army base. What else could mother do? She put socks on everyone. Since they were big wool socks, the two little guys were stuffed in like Christmas toys. The socks made perfect little sleeping bags. The older kids pulled the socks up to their thighs. After father cut holes in the tops, they tied them to their waists.

Lucy and Fay had gotten enough coats for themselves and Bonnie and Stella. Mother wrapped the other blanket around everyone; we were warm enough. Father hooked up a dog team to take us the five miles to the missionaries. The pastor and his wife found us all some clothes from the donation barrels. The pastor let us stay in a small cabin they had for the schoolteacher. We stayed there until father moved us all back to the tide flats in our little duck shack. Father started on a new cabin the next summer with the help of a friend. It was a little sturdier and quite a bit larger than the old one. Sadly, I don't think father's friend was much of a carpenter either. While we stayed in that cabin by the missionary, father put bunk beds outside the cabin by the door. He hung a tarp on the roof logs so that the beds were kind of sheltered between the house and the tarp. The big girls slept outside there under the eaves. They were quick about getting dressed in the morning, because after all, it was winter. The weather would sometimes be thirty below. I don't know how but they stayed warm enough at night with army mummy sleeping bags under that tarp. It didn't take them long to get from their sleeping bags into the house in the morning.

In those days it didn't take people long to finish in the bathroom either, as it was outside plumbing. There was always frost on the outhouse toilet seat in the winter. In the summer, the smell wasn't that great either. That's one part about living in the bush I really don't miss. We had no money, as all of father's furs had burned up in the fire. Father had to hurry out to run his trap line for a couple months more to get enough money to get us through that winter. While staying in that missionary cabin, someone gave us a couple of hand sleds. The older girls spent time sliding on the hills and would sometimes take the younger children for rides. Stella was only six years old and couldn't steer the sled very well, but she got one of the sleds anyway. Stella started sliding down the small hill in front of the cabin. Someone had come looking for father and was talking to mother. He had parked a truck in front of the cabin. Stella rode her hand sled down the little hill and couldn't stop or steer away from the truck. She went under the back of the truck and ran smack into the tail pipe. Her eye was gouged out and hanging onto her cheek. Mother grabbed a clean rag and whetted it to wrap around Stella's face. The man that was there drove mother and Stella to the hospital, where the doctor pushed her eye back in its socket. Stella came home with a bandage over her eye. She had to wear that patch for quite a while. Her eye healed, but her vision was never as good after that.

That wasn't the only accident Stella had while we stayed at that cabin. Mother heated water for baths and laundry as well as for washing dishes on a woodstove. I am not sure how it happened, but a large kettle of boiling water fell off the stove and onto Stella, who had been standing next to the stove to keep warm. Mother grabbed Stella and threw her into the snow bank outside. Mother piled snow over Stella until she cooled off. Stella had about one third of her skin scalded off. Mother treated her with bear grease. It took a long time for Stella to heal from those burns. She still carries the scars today. Most of the children in our family had brands on their backsides as we all stood naked by the stove when we were young. Sooner or later, invariably each child would bend over with his or her backside to the stove. None of us ever learned from our sibling's mistakes. After a few months, father moved us all back to the tide flats.

While we were living at the duck shack that winter, Lucy and Fay had the job of throwing hay to the horses from the haystack. They had to drive a dog team about a mile from home to the hay yard. While going to and from the hay yard each day, they took their gun and hunted for ptarmigan and snowshoe hares. Once Lucy even shot a moose with that .22 rifle. Mother was happy to get the extra meat and hunting also kept the big girls busy, as they couldn't go to school.

There was no way to get to school, because there were no roads out on the flats. During one of the hay runs, the girls stayed out too long hunting and were caught in a blizzard. They couldn't make it home, so turned the dog team loose and burrowed into the haystack. They put the rabbits they had shot on the edge of the haystack so they could get them after the blizzard ended. They had to stay in the haystack all night while they waited for the blizzard to pass. During the night a small fox crawled in the hay near them. It was also trying to keep warm through that blizzard. Lucy and Fay were sure it was a wolf just waiting for them to fall asleep so it could eat them. Lucy held the rifle in her lap just in case the wolf came after them, but it was warm in the hay and even in their fear, they soon fell asleep. In the morning on awaking, the blizzard was gone and so was the little fox and one of the rabbits. I guess he needed breakfast too.

Mother had worried all night after the dogsled had came home with out the girls. Mother put away the dogs, then had all the children on their knees praying half the night. Those big girls had a better night than we did. Mother praised the Lord the next morning when they came walking in for breakfast. During the time we spent in that little shack, Sunday was a special day. A man who lived in Palmer and was a deacon in the church would drive down the ice on the Matanuska slough and take us to church. He only came when the ice was thick enough, but missed very few Sundays. The church gave each of us a new bible. Oh, how we treasured them. Although most of us couldn't read yet, the bibles had beautiful pictures to look at. We made up our own stories as to what was happening in those pictures. I am sure it didn't have a lot to do with the word of God, but they were good stories nevertheless.

Mother read to us out of the bible. She liked to read, but books were in short supply, so she read whatever was available. There was a stack of true detective and other murder magazines that duck hunters had left in the shack. Mother read us stories from the magazines or the bible whichever was handy. We never knew if we would be put to sleep with God or the devil. We were terrorized either way. Sometimes mother would have the older girls read stories to us. That kept us entertained and out from under her feet. They usually used the Sears and Roebuck catalog. They were always new and wonderful stories. Fay read the best stories from that old catalog. We would wrap up in blankets and lay on the shelf beds while she read us stories. She read about those beautiful people, showing us the pictures of their pretty clothes and all the different toys and such. We thought those people must have been kings and queens with all that fancy stuff. They had dishes filled with food we'd never seen before.

Fay gave names to everything, such as apple dumpling pie and orange chicken delight. She had so many wonderfully named dishes. All those catalog children looked so happy. I was sure they were stuffed full of all those treats. We would go to sleep with dreams of living the big catalog life. All the wonderful things we would have. If we could just get one of those Superman suits, we were sure we could fly and accomplish great feats. We tied shirts around our necks and ran and jumped pretending to be Superman. We were great heroes. Surprisingly enough, we never broke our necks jumping out of trees or off the roof to save the world, although we did scare the bejesus out of the livestock on more than one occasion.

While we didn't get our catalog dreams, we did get some toys that winter. During one of the big girls hunting expeditions, they found an old dumpsite. There were many treasures to be had. They brought us a lot of good stuff. Fay gave me a rubber doll that had been slightly damaged; only one side of her head was burned. I loved that doll and had it for many years. They brought Johnny a truck and a rubber cow. The big girls always shared with us little guys. They were so very good to us.

The other toys we got were from father. He went to town a few days before Christmas. To get there, he walked twenty miles across the tide flats with a backpack. He didn't come back right away. On Christmas Eve, a big blizzard came up, and we didn't think he was coming until after Christmas. About seven thirty at night, our lead dog, Slim, started howling. He was right beside the shack, so we could hear him even with the wind blowing. Mother tried to make him stop, but he wouldn't. She hit Slim with the broom, but still he kept on howling. A little while after that, the door burst open and in walked father covered with snow and ice. He had been lost in the blizzard and had walked past the shack. He was headed out to the sea when he heard Slim howling. He followed the sound of Slim's howls until he got home. We were all grateful for Slim after that. Father had gone to a store in Palmer and bargained some fur he trapped for a toy for each child and a ham and canned peaches so mother could make a pie. It was one of the best Christmas times we ever had. We were snug in our little home with good food, and all our family was there.

Hilda with Tanner, our lead sled dog

CHAPTER 3

On Saturday night, it was baths for everyone. That was quite a process. First, all the children were given pails of varying sizes, each pail matching the size of the child. Trips were made to a creek nearby until the big copper boiler was full. The water was heated on the stove or campfire, depending on the time of year. While the water was heating, more water was carried to fill the round galvanized tub half full. After the water was boiling on the stove, the tub was filled with hot water until it was warm enough to get in.

The big girls got a bath first, one at a time. The smaller children were next, and they got in all at once. The water was clean enough for us little guys when we started. It looked more like mud when we got out. I am sure there were times when the smaller children got clean water to begin with, I just can't think of any right now. We really didn't like baths that much anyway. My sister, Fay, liked to comb and braid everyone's hair. I hated to have my hair combed. Fay had to sit on me and hold my arms down with her legs. I would kick and bite, screaming the whole time she was combing. Fay was hardy and persistent and would finish the job. I would just mess up my hair as soon as I got loose anyway. I really don't know why she bothered. I guess she always tried to have us look half civilized. Fay really did care about us little guys more than anyone else.

I remember one time when we got really clean. It was when we first went to the stay at the missionary's place. This was after returning from the tide flats in the spring. Father hadn't rebuilt the house yet. The pastor's wife put us in tubs of very hot water, not boiling. I thought it was close to boiling. With the help of her daughter, we were scrubbed with lye soap and scrub brushes. I think some of my skin might have been scrubbed off with the dirt. I never had to worry about my hair being combed for a while, as they cut it all off. I really don't think we were that dirty, or had lice, but I guess the pastor's wife must have disagreed.

While we were at the missionary's house, I told the pastor that a big dog would come down the hill every day and eat in the dog food barrel. His wife would spank me and tell me I would burn in hell for telling those lies. Yet every day, I continued to tell him the same story, and every day I would get a lecture and a spanking. As we were sitting down to eat dinner one day, I started loudly telling that pastor to look out the window as that big dog is here again eating the dog food right now. He looked, and sure enough, a big black bear was in the dog food barrel helping himself. The pastor got a gun and shot the bear, and they had meat to make sausage. I never got a spanking again for lying about a big dog. I did get tied in the high chair for sucking my thumb though. I guess I must have really liked my thumb, as she would leave me in the high chair for hours with my hands tied to the arms so I couldn't suck my thumb. That was okay though, because I got even later when the pastor's oldest daughter had a birthday. The pastor's wife made a nice birthday cake for her daughter with frosting. I watched her put it on the table from the high chair. She then turned me loose and went outside to get her wash off the line. Big mistake!

She should have left me in the chair if she was going outside. As soon as she went out, I ran to the table and tasted the frosting. I had never had frosting before in my life. It tasted really good. I proceeded to eat the frosting with my hands, making a huge mess and ruining the cake. Well, I was caught with my hands in the proverbial cookie jar. The pastor's wife got a switch and switched me until I had welts from top to bottom. Then she locked me in the attic in a small room where the lady schoolteacher would stay during the school year. That was also a mistake. The pastor's wife had to drive the thirty miles to town to get more cake flour and powdered sugar to make another cake. She was gone an awful long time. After a while I needed to use a potty, but there wasn't a potty up there. I opened every dresser drawer and pottied in each and every one. When the lady got back and came to let me out, she saw what I had done. I was expecting another beating, but she just sat on the bed and cried. Then she sent me to the children's home.

I liked holes in my clothes and was proud my jeans could stand by themselves. They matched the scrapes and scabs on my elbows and knees, of which there were plenty. Dresses were not for me. The skirts got in the way of so many things, like standing on my head and climbing trees. Boy, did I like to climb trees. My brother and I were little monkeys. Or maybe it was Tarzan. We climbed and fought and laughed and climbed some more. There was a willow tree in the front field. It was our tree. Father had planted a tree for each child. The other children got spruce, and Fay got a Birch. We got a wonderful willow. I guess father must have known we would need that tree so full of limbs. It served as he deck of a sailing ship, a tree house in the jungle, and the cockpit of a fighter plane, along with many more fictional places. I went back many years later and sat under that tree and remembered those wonderful times. That tree played a large part in my childhood. The willow is gone now, as it had grown old. Many horses and other animals chewed on its bark and broke the limbs. One spring, it just never came back to life, but it will always live in my memory.

I once had a real nice trike. I have no idea where it came from, only that it was mine, and I rode it everywhere. I usually rode carrying my burnt baby doll with a baby pet goat tied my trike most times. The trike had all the parts except the rubber for the tires. Apparently, rubber tires were not a necessity. The metal rails made for great tracks in the dirt. When the goat got tired of following the trike, she would stop and sit down. As she out weighed me, if she didn't want to go, I couldn't pull her. Sometimes, she would drag me backwards until I turned over. Screaming didn't help me at all. All screaming ever did was just call mother's attention to me, and my goat would be put in a pen or turned loose to join her mother. If the baby were left with her mother all day, we would get no milk for us. I guess that's why mother let me play with the baby goat so much in the first place. Mother needed the milk to cook with, and any extra milk we got after that, we got to drink. After milking the goat, mother would put the milk in a box she had rigged up in the creek to keep it cold. That creek was very cold, so cold your teeth would ache when you drank the water straight out of it. It was really good drinking water though. Not many creeks and streams are clean enough to drink from today.

Mother was the best bread baker in the world. Her cinnamon rolls were tall and fat with butter and raisins on top. Some times we even had walnuts, but not very often as walnuts were hard to get. Those cinnamon rolls were too big to hold in both hands. They tasted so good! Mother always knew when we were coming home from trips to the mountains. She would always have fresh bread and cinnamon rolls keeping warm on the shelf above the stove. We would smell that bread when we were still miles from home. It would be a horse race to get to the house first. The winners got first pick of the food, and winners always picked the biggest rolls with the most raisins or nuts. I had my pick many times. It was always well worth the race.

Mother could put together a meal when there seemed to be nothing in the cupboards. She was amazing. The wonderful meals mother cooked on that old wood stove, moose or caribou roasts with potatoes, carrots and onions. Not a lot of spices were needed. Roast brisket was everyone's favorite. We could clean up a whole brisket in one meal. After all there were eight children. We all loved boiled moose tongue, and bone marrow soup was always a big hit. I still cook that when I can get marrowbones, but nothing cooks like a woodstove or a Dutch oven on the coals. When mother fried steak or potatoes, she used a very large cast iron fry pan she had inherited from Grandma Luster. She had to cook a large amount of food at once to feed all the children and extra folk whom seemed to show up at that time of day. We always shared what we had. That was how we lived. My mother and father taught us that we should never send anyone away from our door hungry.

I also inherited that frying pan. When it became too heavy for me, I passed it to my son. He uses it in his home today. We had ham baked in it last Thanksgiving. It seems to cook better with each generation. My son, Kenneth, is very pleased to have that big pan. I guess it will pass to one of his children someday.

With so many creeks, lakes, and rivers fishing was a large part of our lives. We even caught fish with our hands. We would spend time lying on a creek bank trailing both our hands in the water, one hand behind the fish and one in front. You just slowly back the fish up through your hand until your fingers slip into the gill slits. Then, you jerk them out. There was dinner. Sometimes when we didn't have a hook, we would bend a safety pin and use it. You just have to jerk the fish right out as soon as it gets on the line, or it will get away. The only fishing rule was if you catch fish, you clean them so they can be cooked. No waste of food was allowed. We also fed fish to the dogs at times. Mother or father cooked the fish with rice in a big pot over a fire for the dogs.

Johnny and I would tie burlap, gunny bags on our horse saddles and ride to a good fishing hole. We would fill those bags with fish in a couple of hours. We then had to clean them all, which was not our favorite part. Mother always cooked what we caught. We were served fish cooked in many ways. If we caught enough to make a batch, father would smoke them. Fish are very tasty that way. We would eat smoked fish like candy, which is what smoked or dried fish is called in Alaska (Eskimo candy). Father also smoked the fish he brought home from coastal hunting trips. Many kinds of very ugly fish were brought home; all were smoked. I don't remember if there was any difference in taste. I just know they all tasted good.

After smoking a huge batch of sea fish from one such trip, maybe a couple hundred pounds, father left them on the racks in the smokehouse to dry for a couple weeks. Smoked fish has to dry so it doesn't mold. While they were drying, we were raiding the racks. When father went to check on the progress, he was a very unhappy man. Most of the fish were gone. He called all of us together for a lecture and ended with a swat on the backside for each child. The next time he smoked fish, we ate most of those also. He knew we would. They were just too good not too.

I made a safety pin hook one summer day and was wildly swinging it around. I caught my biggest catch ever, my little sister. I hooked her right under the chin. Well, I had her halter broke in no time. Mother promptly grabbed an ear and halter broke me too. I never went fishing that day, as my backside was too sore from the warming it got from mother and her willow switch. You know, I really never got any spankings I didn't deserve. I'm sure I did something that warranted the spanking, even if I didn't think so at that moment.

At sometime during that fall, mother went away for a couple of days, leaving Johnny and I in charge. Johnny and I really out did ourselves. We had a baby sister, Norma. She was very small, not even crawling yet. I think she was only a month or two old. She slept in a cardboard Carnation milk box. We were to feed and take care of her. Really I don't remember feeding or changing her, but we must have. If we did feed her, she got milk poured straight out of a carnation milk can and into a dirty bottle. I guess like Stella, Norma must have been tough too.

While mother was away, we got bored and went looking for something to do. We decided to play with the guns. We got all of the guns down from the wall and took most of them outside. One shotgun we tied to a sawhorse and aimed towards some chickens that were in the yard. I think we missed. I least I hope so. I think we fired most of the guns in one way or another.

We were putting them all back so we wouldn't get in trouble when Johnny pressed the 30-06 into little sister's tummy. He pulled the trigger. Thank God it didn't go off. Just then the dogs started barking, and we knew some one was coming. We hurried to get the rest of the guns back, the last one being the 30-06. When I put it back on the wall, my finger must have hit the trigger. It went off and shot a hole in the roof. I guess Johnny just had not pulled hard enough on the trigger earlier. Mother raced into the house when she heard that shot and boy were we in trouble. We never told her about the gun pointed at my little sister, or we would have been dead for sure.

When Johnny turned five years old, father gave him a very small .22 caliber single shot rifle. At that time, father gave me a pump .22 rifle. I was older and had a little hunting behind me, so I kept all the bullets. Father sent us out to find some spruce hens, also called grouse. I was supposed to help Johnny shoot a spruce hen. They are stupid birds and don't fly away. We found some birds at the lower end of the horse pasture in some spruce trees. I gave Johnny one bullet, but didn't wait for him to shoot the bird like I was told to do. I guess I was being a smart aleck.

Instead, I quickly shot the nearest bird, and the others went behind the tree. Johnny couldn't see them and started crying, because he was angry with me. He then turned and shot at me. I ran home and told father. Johnny lost his gun for a month, and so did I. We both got a butt warming too. Johnny was spanked for shooting at me, and I got spanked for not following father's orders. I really deserved to get the same treatment as Johnny, as I was a brat. Good thing I never gave Johnny more bullets. He could load a rifle pretty fast. Most of the time, we were the best of buddies. We are only nine months apart in age. Johnny was a premature baby and stayed small through those early years. I was small also but more robust and tough. I protected him back then, and later he returned the favor.

We moved into an old bus while father was building the new house. It was fixed up like a camper with table and benches, icebox, cook stove that ran on propane, and a bedroom in the back. There was a little wood stove by the front door to heat the bus. There was a door at the back as well. It was the first place we ever lived that had two doors. When they finished the floor on the new house, the logs were only three logs high. One of the older girls nailed the neighbor boy to the floor. They carefully nailed his clothes all the way around him, not wanting to hurt him. After they had him secured, they went to play somewhere else, forgetting about him. About suppertime, the boy's father came looking for him because he was told to be home by then. When ask about him, the girls had to confess where they had left him. Boy, were they in trouble!

We all played in the new house during construction. It was made of spruce logs, which were full of spruce beetles. Those are some very scary looking bugs to a five year old. I was crawling along the top of the wall when I ran into a beetle. It was crawling along just like me, minding its own business. I panicked, screamed, promptly passed out, and fell off the wall. I woke up with a split open head and swore the beetle did it. No one could convince me otherwise. I have disliked bugs ever since. I had tonsillitis shortly after that bug issue, so I went to the children's home for a while where they gave me antibiotics. Thankfully they never took my tonsils out. I still have them.

While I was there, some people took me home to adopt me, but soon returned me, as I was too wild. I was having fun at their house too. They sent me to church daycare during the day to do crafts and play with other children. After daycare, I would go home and play in the yard or street by their house. One day a boy about my size was playing in the street. He started throwing small pieces of gravel towards me.

I guess I took it wrong and tackled him. I dragged him to a vacant lot next door and tied him to a fence with some twine I had in my pocket. I went back to playing in the street until called in for dinner. I forgot about that boy, or perhaps I just didn't care. I don't remember. About one o'clock in the morning, the people woke me up because someone remembered the little boy playing near me earlier that day. Everyone including the cops had been looking for that poor little boy. I told them yes, I had seen that little boy, and far as I knew he was still tied to the fence, which he was. The poor little guy had cried himself to sleep. After that, I guess they didn't want to adopt me because I went back to the children's home.

Fay with Mopsy

CHAPTER 4

Father homesteaded in a beautiful valley between King Mountain and Castle Mountains in a fertile lake bottom that had drained out ages before he got there. Oats grew six feet high on our forty-acre hay field. Blue grass grew thick and knee deep in the meadows and horses pastures. The high grass bordered the creek that wandered through the valley. Landlocked salmon would swim up from the lake to spawn in the creek. Snowshoe hare and other small game and birds abounded in the valley. There were also predators: wolves, coyotes, bears and Canadian lynx. Many birds of prey sailed overhead. Moose and caribou were abundant in the surrounding hills and river valleys. White Dall sheep and mountain goats dotted the walls and cliffs of near by ridges. Many hours were spent watching the sheep and goats through father's field glasses and many more hours in trying to catch those wild lambs. None were ever caught.

Our livestock had to wear bells on their necks to keep from being eaten. Wolves and bears don't like the clanging sound. The bells also helped us to find the horses and cows when they wandered off. We could just listen, and most of the time, some of them could be heard. We would know which animals were where by the sound of the bells. Each bell sounds different.

Mother had a hard time keeping chickens, even with wire runs. They were taken by coyotes, lynx, and sometimes killed by weasels. Coyotes would dig under the fence during the night, if someone had forgotten to close the chicken house door in the evening. Morning would arrive with very few chickens. It had happened more than once. Wild predators took some of our horses, but horse thieves also stole many too. Father branded the horse with a hot iron, but that didn't stop the thieves. One year a colt of mine was taken. Five years later, I bought him back for $500. That really was a pretty good deal, as he came back gelded and saddle and pack trained. I couldn't have fed him and trained him nearly so cheaply. I was thinking, maybe that horse thief would like to do the same with a couple more. I told him so, but it was not appreciated. I was a rather mouthy kid. Most of the horses that were stolen never did come back. Only a few were recovered, and those were mostly from people who had taken them to go hunting, or for just a short ride.

Father had workhorses that were used to plow fields and pull wagons and sleds. Father hauled supplies in a horse drawn wagon in summer and with a horse or dog sled in winter. Father would let the little kids ride on the workhorses' backs. We would climb up the harness like a ladder, then hold onto the brass knobs on the collar. We thought we were driving. The horses never even seemed to notice we were up there. We kicked our legs, looking like small windmills, wanting the horses to go faster. I don't think the horses paid us much attention. They never went any faster. Sometimes, we hauled water with the big bobsled, using steel milk cans of ten and twenty-gallon sizes. Water would be dipped out of the creek with a bucket until all the cans were full. The lids were then placed on the milkman, and the water was pulled home to fill the fifty gallon barrels in the house. This was done at least once a week. Our most dependable workhorse was a cream draft mare named Polly. She was very gentle and knew where to go for water and wood. She could tell which place we were going by what equipment she was hooked up to.

When I was six, father let me take Polly all by myself to get water. It never went quite as I had envisioned it. It started out good, Polly took me right to the waterhole and stopped while I got my bucket and filled all the cans. Things were looking good. I put on all the lids and was ready to go home. That was when things changed. I got in the sled and told Polly let's go home, just as father did. Polly never moved a muscle. I begged her to go home. Nothing. I yelled at her using every colorful name I had ever heard father call a horse, still nothing. I walked to her head and pulled on her bridle as hard as I could, telling her every awful thing I was going to do to her if she didn't move. Still nothing. I had enough by then. I started crying as I found a big stick. That was when father stumbled out from behind the tree where he had been watching the whole time. He was laughing so hard he could hardly stand up. Polly's ears went straight up when she saw father, and she started for home. Father yelled whoa, so we could get aboard. We both rode home. That old mare knew she had me buffaloed, but not father. She never did that to me again. I guess she expected to see father step out from behind a tree if she did.

Polly stayed with us for many years. She gave us many fine foals. I think her best was a pale palomino colt my sister Fay named Major. My father had him for twenty-six years. He was kept a stallion and became our best herd sire. Two of my sisters still have some of his great-grandchildren. They are used for riding and packing in the mountains. Fay has a trail-riding outfit. She rides those same trails we used growing up. Father made hundreds of miles of trails all through the mountains. Stella now has a gold mine in those same mountains. Not much gold, but she hauls out gemstones and spends her winters making jewelry to sell.

I spent many hours lying on Polly's broad back, daydreaming while she grazed. She really was a gentle old soul and tolerated the small children climbing her legs and looking up her nostrils. She was always careful not to step on any of us. On the other hand, I have seen her step on a man's foot and lean into it, moving every foot but the one he was hollering about. She knew we were babies and that's why she was so patient.

In the fall when the berries were ripe, mother made jam. All the children were sent to pick berries. Mother made tiny buckets for the smallest of us. The biggest girls had two gallon lard buckets. The middle girls had three pound coffee cans, and the little guys had peach cans with wire handles mother had made from baling wire. We always ate a lot of berries before we filled our buckets, that saved mother from having to stop the jam making process to make us lunch. Mother made many kinds of jams and jellies for winter. She picked the strawberries herself to save her plants from our little feet and hands. The rest were made from wild berries, raspberries, high-bush cranberries, black and red currants, and salmon berries. The blueberries were picked later, and we had to ride up the mountain a little ways for them. After a day of making jam, mother always made baking powder biscuits so we could eat some of the new jam. There were always some leftovers from jar filling. Mother sure made good jam.

Mother washed our clothes on a washboard after we were covered with jam. When we were tall enough to reach the top of the tub, we helped wash our own clothes. Therefore, it made us happy when father made enough money one year to buy mother a gas driven washing machine. That sure helped mother, except she washed more often and that meant more water for us to haul. It was nice that we had cleaner clothes. The new washing machine had a wringer on top that you ran the clothes through to help dry. It squeezed out the water between rollers. It was very dangerous. There was a release on top to hit if you got stuck in the rollers. The problem was you had to be able to reach the release and hit it hard enough to get it to open. Once, Lucy's hand got caught in the wringer and got rolled all the way to the elbow before mother could get it open. Her arm wasn't broken, but it did swell up pretty badly for a while. After that event, none of the children were allowed near the washing machine while it was running.

The dryer was always a clothesline. I was jerked off a horse more than once going under it. The line hit me right under the chin when I was on a horse. I was usually under the clothesline, because the horse was running away. It certainly wasn't on purpose. Mother didn't care. She would use the broom on the horse and me if her laundry hit the ground. The clothesline was strung between the back of the house and the outhouse. That outhouse was the best building on the place. It was a beauty. It had three holes and a trough for the boys. It also had a window to look out and an extra chair just in case you had to wait. There was a hitching post to tie up your horse while you went too. Come to think of it, maybe father never built that out house.

Everyone that came to stay for a while built a shack. Soon we had a lot of small shacks around the property. Maybe one of those people built the outhouse. As the children reach the age of twelve or thereabouts, they would move into one of the shacks. The younger children only stayed in the shacks in the summer, but the older girls lived in them year around. Lucy and Fay had cook stoves in their shacks to help keep warm. They would cook food for us little guys if we asked, and ask we did. Fay made pies and cookies. Lucy only made tapioca pudding. Someone gave her a few cases of tapioca so she made it every day there for a long time. In spite of it, amazingly I still like tapioca today.

We had chickens so we also had eggs. We ate a lot of eggs. Even us little guys could boil an egg. Stella could whip the whites up as fast as I have ever seen it done. Then she added sugar and vanilla, making a topping for all that tapioca. The older girls married early. I think they were only sixteen. I don't think their lives improved much till much later. They all had babies right away, and there went their teenage years. I don't think they have ever known anything but hard work. We all grew up in a hard life, but we didn't know it, so were basically happy. We thought we had it made. After all we had horses to ride, dogs to use on the sleds, and trees to climb. What more could you want? We couldn't care less that our clothes were rags. The lack of shoes only mattered in the winter. We usually had hand-me-down shoes from the donation barrel at the church. If the shoes were too big, it was all the better, as you could get on more socks. We always had plenty of socks. They came from the army base and were big, thick wool socks. You could pull them over your pants legs to above the knee.

We always were into something, as are most children. When Lucy and Fay were small, they found mother's workbasket. She had all her sewing stuff in it, including her scissors. Well, you can probably guess what happened next. Lucy bobbed off all of Fay's hair in hunks. Mother tried to straighten it out, but there was not much left to work with. It took a while to look better. Father started calling her Bobby Fay. She hated that name. She would pout in a corner when called that name. This is what mother told me, since I was not born yet. Lucy was the main one to start things, but only from the background. Therefore, we were usually the ones getting caught and getting the punishment. Lucy was the one hiding and laughing at us. I guess all big sisters and brothers do that?

When we didn't get caught, Lucy was the one reaping the benefits of whatever she sent us to do, like raiding the garden. When we would be discovered, she would yell, "Run, run!" But mother was a fast runner and would usually catch us. When we got older and could run faster, mother would just wait until we forgot about things, then she would catch us. When we were really in trouble,

44

mother made us pick our own willow switch. Now, you may think that it helped, us picking a switch that wouldn't hurt as much. But, you'd be wrong. We had to pick a good one. If we picked one that was to dry and broke or too little, mother would use it on us until it broke. Then she would pick a real long one that wrapped around and whack us with that a few times. I learned to pick thicker ones and as short as we could get away with, because if the willow switches were to long or to pliable, they hurt more, leaving bigger welts and lasting longer. The longer switches would wrap around you and leave welts in the front as well as the back. The thicker ones hurt just as much when you were being hit, but they didn't leave welts, only bruises. Bruises didn't hurt much later like welts did. Mother kept us fairly under control. Well, maybe not for civilized people, but we weren't city folks. We lived a very free life, devoid of rules and regulations for the most part. It was a life we will never live again. It's a different world now. In spite of everything, we all grew up healthy of mind and body and content with our lives, which is more than most children can count on in today's world.

We would spend most of our summers in the mountains, getting camps repaired for fall hunting and living a nomadic life. Hunting, fishing, and bathing in the rivers are how we lived. We hunted for gemstones, stacking them in piles to be brought out and sold later. There were many ways us children helped the family earn a living. Everyone was happy to share the work. There are a lot of food items in the hills and mountains too, if you know where to find them. Father taught us from toddlers how to survive in the woods. One of the best things we learned was which mushrooms were edible and which to leave alone. As we were going from one place to another, father would pick mushrooms and other edible plants. He would put them in the front of his shirt until his shirt was so full he looked like Santa. He would instruct us as he picked each plant. When we stopped at the next camping spot, father would show us how to prepare whatever he had found.   When it was mushrooms, he always made gravy and baking powder biscuits. We loved them. One summer father sent a few of the children with a hired hand into the Sheep Valley to fix camps. It was a miserable trip, raining every day with no food and no wood. The only food we had was a bag of pancake mix and two jars of mothers jam. We were there a couple of weeks. Believe me, we were tired of pancakes and jam. Besides we could only have a little jam as it had to last until something else came along. The only firewood was from very small bushes that grew in the high valley.

The children spent most of the days gathering sticks so we could have a fire at night and cook our pancakes. In order to cook, we had to pack foam rubber in a food can as tightly as you could. That would last long enough and get hot enough to cook on. Relief came early one morning before we were awake. A curious moose came and stuck his head into our tent. The hired man jumped up, grabbing his gun. We finally had meat. As soon as the moose was down, the two big girls ran out to butcher it. We little guys started building a fire to cook stick meat, which is just meat held over a fire on a stick. That was some of the best moose meat I've ever had, but of course we all loved fresh stick meat anyway.

Father showed up a few days later and brought food for the rest of the trip. We were finished there, so we moved on to the next camp that needed repair. The next place was in a river valley. There we also had fish to eat. There were trees in the valley to camp under too, so it was much dryer. We also had plenty of wood. Everyone warmed up after the second camp. With father there, us smaller children had less to do, so we played more. We all fattened up on the moose meat. It was a lot more fun, and we weren't hungry the rest of the trip.

One of my sisters playing

CHAPTER 5

In the fall of 1955, father took us all up the Oshetna River to hunt caribou. Each person was allowed five caribou in those days. Each child counted as a person, as long as he or she could hold a rifle. Of course we didn't really shoot the caribou, father did that, but we had to be there to be counted as a person to get the caribou. A lot of things went wrong on that trip. First the saddle that Johnny and I were sharing slipped under the belly of the horse we were riding. We got shook up, but nothing too bad. It was a miracle, as the horse we were riding was kind of crazy. His name was Glass Eyes, as he had white eyes. He was known for spooking and kicking every thing in sight. If you hit him on the butt, he would back up real fast. If you hit him on the shoulder, he would go forward. We had been riding four or five hours, and he was as tired as were we. Father stopped the pack string and came back when the big girls started yelling. Father pulled us from under Glass Eyes, put the saddle back on, and lifted us back up top, and we were off again. All the children were tired and kept asking father when we would get there. His answer was always the same, "Just around this next hill."

Five hills later, Fay who had been riding asleep with her legs crossed over the saddle horn, fell off. When she landed, her face hit a large rock. She split open her head and broke her cheekbone. She just got right back on and wouldn't let father look at her. She was one tough little cookie. By the time father decided to camp for the night, Fay's face was badly swollen. She just said nothing, and father couldn't do anything anyway. There was no way to patch her up. I guess she lost weight, as she couldn't eat much for a while after that. Mostly, she just drank meat broth. I don't think she had much weight to spare though. Fay was a very tiny little thing.

After a few days we finally got to where the caribou were traveling through. All the children were worn out from days of riding and being cold. It probably wasn't all that long, but when you are only five, every day seems like forever. For most of that first day in base camp, the little guys didn't even get out of their sleeping bags. They were just trying to keep warm. It was raining all day and frosting hard at night. Everything was wet, frozen, or both.

Father turned the horses loose in a canyon to feed for a few days while he hunted caribou. Each day Lucy or Fay would go to the canyon to get one of the horses to pack meat into camp. They always used a different horse so the horses would all have a chance to rest up for the long trip home. Each day, father would shoot seven or eight caribou as close to camp as possible. The location made it easier and faster for mother and the big girls to butcher the caribou and bring the meat back to camp. The smaller children had the job of collecting firewood. As wood became scarce near camp, we had to go farther out each day to get enough for cooking fires.

I was quite far from camp collecting wood when I saw Lucy a short way up the hill from me. She called me up to see a caribou she was preparing to butcher. It had been shot but was not quite dead, still moving its head. When I got to where Lucy was standing, she decided to scare me. She started yelling at me, "Run, it's going to get you!" Well, that scared me. I ran as fast as I could down the mountain. As I ran around a rock, there was another caribou lying between camp and me. I thought it was the same one, and it was after me. I changed direction and ran toward the canyon wall. I ran right into another dead caribou. I went into a bigger panic and ran over the canyon wall and into the canyon. Lucky for me, it was not overly steep in that spot. I got down safely. When I got to the bottom, I started looking for a place to hide. I found a hole behind some rocks where a porcupine had wintered. I was real small. I barely fit in that hole. I wedged myself as far back as I could get. I was just able to peek out a few feet in front of the hole. Lucy told father her version of what had happened. She said the caribou had scared me, and I ran in the direction of the canyon, leaving her wicked part out of the tale.

Everyone spent hours looking for me. I heard them calling my name, but I knew it was the caribou calling me out so they could get me. I was no fool. I stayed tight in my hole. Those caribou weren't going to trick me like that. Everyone looked all day and late into the evening. They couldn't find me. Father got horses saddled to make the long run back to civilization so he could get help to find me. The army had a search and rescue unit that would come on such calls. Father was very upset over the whole fiasco, as not only was I missing, but also the hunting had stopped. We needed that meat for winter. There was a man named Sam Moore who was hunting with us. He kept searching for me even when everyone else had given up. He walked that canyon calling me for hours. I heard him, but I knew it was one of those caribou just tricking me. He happened to walk close enough to my hole that I saw his boots and Levi pants legs. I was out of that hole in a flash and climbed him like a tree. He carried me out of that canyon. Well, he had to carry me, as he couldn't get me off his neck. He was my hero. He had saved me from the caribou. He called me Caribou Kate after that. He also saved the hunting trip. Father was happy that he never had to stop hunting. Lucy was not so happy after I told father what had really happened. I think he kicked her butt around camp a bit.

That winter we moved to a Quonset hut on Fishhook Road just outside of Palmer. It was a really great house. It had electric lights and an inside toilet! The first indoor toilet we ever had. There was running water, not running water from a nearby a creek. There were even four bedrooms. It was the first time every one in the family was not in the same room. I thought we must have gotten rich. Father had rented the fields for the livestock, and the house went with them. We all got to go to school. A bus came right at the end of the driveway. Best of all, the house had an oil stove, which meant no wood to chop or haul into the house. Mother had an electric stove to cook on.

There was another Quonset hut connected to the one we were living in. Some young men that were working for father lived in one end of it. Some baby calves were penned in the other end. They were so cute. They were jersey cows and looked like what I thought a deer looked like. I thought father had brought home Bambi. Everything was wonderful. Christmas came and went. Mother got new fancy moccasins. Every child got a fancy new Hudson Bay blanket. I got a new pair of Red Wing leather boots. I hung them on the wall to look at, as they were too pretty and too good to wear. We were all as happy as could be.

On New Year's night the Quonset that the boys lived in caught fire. I don't know how the fire started; maybe a calf knocked a light into the straw. The fire was well out of control by the time it was discovered. Mother was trying to get all the children out. Father was not there. Lucy tried to save the calves. I think she saved one or two. Fay started throwing all our new blankets out the back window. Little Johnny crawled up on the kitchen counter and got hold of the zenith radio, trying to get it off the wall. He was hanging onto it swinging from a nail when some one came by and scooped him up, radio and all. He saved it and still has it today. I got my new boots off the wall and climbed under the bed to hide from the fire. When Fay pulled the blanket off the bed she found me. She pulled me out from under there and threw me out the window. She jumped out behind me just as the whole house went up in flames. Fay saved me and most of the blankets.

Well, there went the nice house. It was back to the cabin in Chickaloon. We didn't go back to school that year either. The two oldest girls spent the rest of the winter on the trap line with father. The next winter we spent at a cabin on Faulk Road near Palmer so the children could go to school. It was back to primitive living, hauling water by sled and chopping wood, just like at our homestead. We had to walk two miles down the road to catch the school bus. I only went to school half a year, the year before so I could not read. Instead of being placed in the second grade, I had to go to progressive first grade, which was the greatest thing that ever happened to me. I learned to read. Reading opened whole new worlds for me. I read everything I could get my hands on. I escaped into books. You could always find me in some corner hiding in a book. I have never lost my love of books.

That year I also got my very fist pair of new girl's shoes. I had been wearing a pair of shoes given to me by someone that were pretty much used up. A nail from the heel was sticking through the bottom and into my foot. The first grade teacher saw me walking funny and investigated the reason. When she saw it was a nail in my shoe, she sent me down to the boiler room so the janitor could pull it out. The janitor looked at the shoes, and then had me wait on a chair there in the boiler room while he went to talk to the principal. When he came back, he had my coat and hat. He took me to the co-op store and let me try on shoes. I picked a pair of shiny bright red Mary Jane shoes. I was so excited, and they were so beautiful. What a nice and caring man that janitor was.

Small Moccasin Tracks

Johnny and I played and explored the mountains and valleys around the whole area. We were always off somewhere in the woods. After about eight years old, we spent most of our time away from home. Many days and sometimes a week or two would be spent in the woods by ourselves. Nobody ever looked for us, unless they needed the horses we had. Of course there was one time when we took two of the neighboring farm children with us that people came looking. Father tracked us to a camp a few miles up the Kings River. We really got ourselves in trouble that time. I guess those children had parents that worried about them. They weren't raised in the woods like us. We were forbidden to ever take anyone with us again. The willow welts on my back kept me convinced for a long time.

The neighbor farm girl was the same age as me; we became good friends. We are still friends today. We tried our first cigarettes together. She got two cigarettes from her mother's pack. They were safely hidden where we played in a log pile. Then forgotten. For two years those cigarettes stayed there through summer rains and winter snows. They had turned hard and brown when we rediscovered them. That was when we decided to try smoking cigarettes. We thought they were nice and well aged. After lighting them, we tried to smoke them, but I think we may have lost half a lung coughing. We coughed until tears made tracks down our dirty little faces. I was so sick and wretched for a while. I guess Vicky was a little hardier. She never got sick. Thankfully that was my first and last experience with a cigarette. I never took up smoking again. I thought anything that made you feel that bad couldn't possibly be good for you.

Memories of an Alaskan Mountain Family

When Johnny and I were older, maybe around nine years old, we went to the movies for the first time. We watched a western of some sort. I think it may have been High Noon. After seeing the movie, we would play sheriff and robbers with the neighbor children. As we had the horses, we were always the law. We used the little shacks that were scattered around as our town. It was a lot of fun. First the bank, which was the goat house, had to be robbed. Next, we'd rob the general store (the chicken house). Then like any good robber, we would ride away. Then the law would have to chase down the robbers and have shootouts with our stick guns. We would tie the robbers up and take them to jail in the saddle shed. Our game was great fun until we thought up new stuff to do to those robbers. We decided to drag the robbers back to jail behind the horses, not a very well thought out idea I might add as it turned out. Father heard the little robbers crying and came to see what we were up to. Apparently, we didn't have the brains that God gave a damn goose, because people can get dragged to death if the horses spooked and ran off. We were also told people could also be disfigured or crippled for life playing like that. Anyway, Father ended our game with a whack of the willow switch for each of us, expect for the crying robbers. Father thought they'd had enough punishing from the dragging. Although none of those little robbers were seriously hurt, I can't say the same for Law's backsides. I don't think we could sit down for a day or so. We spent the rest of the summer being cowboys instead, trying to rope the goats, pigs, and chickens with little much success I might add. Do you know how hard it is to rope a chicken?

Small Moccasin Tracks

That year we went to school at the Old Missionary School. It became state funded and a public school. There were eleven children that went to the Old Missionary School; most of them were from our family. We rode horses to school in the fall. The horses were tied to trees during the school day. We each brought a bundle of oat hay behind our saddles. At first recess the horses were led to the creek to drink, then fed their hay. After school we would race home to do our chores. There was no shortage of chores. Wood always needed to be split and brought in; dogs and horses needed to be feed, and the chickens also needed food and water. In the chicken house, we had to light lamps to keep them warm at night and on cold days. We did our homework by lamplight too.

When Halloween came around, we all dressed up in costumes for school that day. I dressed as a hobo. I had a red handkerchief tied on a stick over my shoulder. What the teacher didn't know was that I had spent time early that morning gathering mice from under the oat shocks. My hobo pack had eight or ten mice in it. I put one in the teacher's top desk drawer. The rest went in the closet in a box. Well, of course the teacher found her surprise first. Meanwhile the other mice had chewed their way out of the box in the closet. They started running all around the classroom. The teacher climbed her desktop and cried. Her husband came in and swept the mice out the door with the broom. We were all laughing, for a while anyway. Then I got in trouble for bringing the mice. The teacher was yelling at me and pointing her finger in my face. I just grabbed her finger and bit it all the way to the bone. He husband came in to spank me. I wasn't having any of that either. Every time he hit me, I hit him back. Then the big girls came to my rescue. They backed that man off me. We all ran for the horses and high tailed it out of there.

Father had to go down to the school and straighten things out. He told the teacher he was going to give me a whipping, but he never did. I think he got a lot of amusement out of the whole thing. He talked about it for years. That teacher quit, and we had to go back to walking the five miles to the bus stop to go to the Central School in Palmer. We caught the bus in the dark at seven in the morning and rode thirty-two miles to school. We got off in the dark at five thirty in the afternoon. The bus driver would leave the lights on so we could do our homework on the bus. He was a real nice man.

The little guys would fall asleep on the bus on the way home. Once my youngest sister, Norma, fell asleep, and we forgot her on the bus. The bus driver found her when he was sweeping out the bus at the end of his shift. He drove her all the way home to our road, then pulled her on a small sled the five miles to our house. He met mother walking down our road. She was heading to town all those miles away to find Norma. Mother was so relieved to see the bus driver with Norma. We always made sure to wake the little ones after that. We never got in trouble with mother, but we'd been really scared mother would freeze in the snow on that long walk to Palmer. Thanks to the bus driver, everything turned out all right.

In those days you only had to attend school until you reached the sixth grade or turned sixteen. Lucy must have reached one or both, as she was out of school at that time. Most of us were behind in school since we didn't go that often. As it was, Lucy would be sent by mother to pick us up with the dog team at the bus stop. Sometimes if she got there early, she would hide and scare us. She got a lot of laughs making us cry and run. We couldn't tell mother what Lucy was doing, as she threatened to not pick us up anymore if we did, and we believe her.

One good thing about Central School was they had free lunch for us. We all loved the hot food we got there. I always wrapped up some extra food for the bus ride home for my two little sisters. It was a long time from lunch until we got home. Stella always had a box of milk in her pocket. If the little ones didn't drink the milk, Stella made ice cream with it later. She put it outside, and after it got slushy she added sugar and vanilla. It was really good ice cream.

Mother had a hard time with her chickens. Even though they were locked up most of the time, something was stealing them. Mother thought it might be a lynx or coyote. I am sure they did take some. The hawks and owls took their share as well. On this day, when Johnny and I were sent to gather eggs, the thief was something else. Johnny went in first and started yelling about a big animal in the chicken house. He came out faster than he went in. I grabbed a big stick, really so big I could hardly swing it. I stayed to save the chickens. I went in the chicken coop and closed the door so the animal couldn't get away and started hitting it with my stick.

Johnny ran to get mother. Our house was a good two hundred yards from the chicken house. By the time Johnny got to the house, he was out of breath and not making much sense. The only thing mother understood was a lynx or bear or something was killing Hilda in the chicken house. Mother got the shotgun, and with Lucy and Fay in tow, she ran to save me. When mother opened that chicken house door, her and the big girls went to gagging.

Memories of an Alaskan Mountain Family

I had chased that poor little pine weasel all around the chicken house hitting it with every jump. Weasels are members of the skunk family. It had sprayed up that chicken house with so much scent, you could hardly see for the tears. Mother sat on the ground outside and laughed so hard she couldn't get up. I think the weasel escaped out the door at the earliest opportunity. It was just there to have an egg for lunch, and lunch was over. Mother did tell us not to do anything like that again, but of course that went in one ear and out the other.

The big girls teased us for quite some time after that. They called us mighty hunters and told everyone who happen to come by what we had done, but hey, we just little children. Unfortunately, it took a while to get that smell off me. The chickens were hard to get back in the chicken house at night for a while after that too. But, it was soon forgotten, as new adventures were happening everyday, some good, and some not so much. We all learned to live and take care of each other. Everyone had to do their share and look after those younger than themselves. We took those lessons to heart and have always lived with a strong family bond.

Lucy, Bonnie, Fay with Tanner the sled dog

CHAPTER 6

We had a lot of horses. We rode them all, if we could climb on. We had many ways to do that. If the horse had a long mane, we would grab the mane and put our feet on the horse's knee to repel up to the back. Sometimes we had to trick the horses to get on. We would get them near a fence or rock that was tall enough for us to get on. Some of the horses got wise to our tricks and wouldn't stand broadside to anything. Most of the time, we just climbed on and went wherever the horse wanted to go, because we didn't always have a bridle. As we got older, we learned to make the horses go where we wanted, with or with out a bridle or halter. If even one person had a bridle that worked fine, as all the horses would follow the lead horse.

Memories of an Alaskan Mountain Family

Sometimes all the horses would be gone. That's when I started riding a black and white bull calf, named Bully. I saddled him, put on a bridle, and off we would go. He walked real slow, but we went everywhere anyway. I had to walk up or down any steep hills, as the saddle wouldn't stay on very well. Bully never steered very well either. I could pull his head all the way around till it was resting on my knee, and he would still go straight if he took a notion. He finally got too big and bullish for me to ride, and father took him away.

Father replaced Bully with a Shetland pony. In fact, father bought four Shetland ponies that year, one for each of us little guys. Norma got a tiny black gelding named Friday. He was too little for a bigger person to get on and teach him any thing. She always had to be led behind another pony, because Friday didn't steer. My little sister got a beautiful red and white gelding named Sparky. He was only two years old, but a real people pleaser. Johnny got a real cute and very sturdy white gelding with a black head. Johnny named him Jug Head. Jug Head was a great pony that everyone could ride, but I got the best pony.

My pony was a beautiful chocolate gelding with a white mane and tail. I named him Silver of course. He was the most beautiful pony in the world. Silver like me had a bit of an attitude at times. He bucked me off every time I wasn't paying attention, and sometimes when I was. Sometimes he would bite and kick me. I loved Silver. I was sure he looked just like an Arabian stallion. He was the king of the wind in my mind. I saved up five dollars to buy a pair of fancy spurs I'd seen at the feed store. They were really pretty with engraved sides and real pointy rowels. I really wanted those spurs.

I gave my five dollars to father when he went to get supplies the next time. I waited all day and into the evening hoping the spurs hadn't been sold to someone else. When father got home, it was early evening. He'd brought those spurs. I was so excited as I strapped the spurs on. I was quite proud of myself. I sauntered out to my pony, looking like Rowdy Yates I was sure. Father was standing around with some hunting clients and hired hands watching me. I thought they were impressed with me in my spurs. I really put on the strut then. I swaggered over and jumped on Silver with a flourish. What I didn't know was father had told them what to expect, and they were waiting for me to make a fool of myself.

I raked those spurs down Silvers sides, just like I had seen in the movies. He didn't moved. What I didn't notice in my excitement was that Silver had tightened up every muscle in his body. I touched him again with those spurs to move him forward. The next thing I knew, I was sailing through the air. I landed on my head in a heap right in front of all those people, which was what everyone was waiting to see. They all had a good laugh at my expense. I was totally humiliated. I took those spurs off right there and handed them to the nearest person. In my humiliation, I swore never to wear spurs again. I never have. There was never a need to wear spurs. My horses have always worked for me, because they wanted to please me. That is the way it should be. I always rode the horses that were the wildest. They bucked me off many times, but I just got right back on. I always had an understanding with the horses. If I could stay on, I could ride them. When they became to tame for me, they were passed on to someone else.

Memories of an Alaskan Mountain Family

My older sister, Fay, was the real dare devil of the family. She rode the real rough stock. The harder they bucked, the more she liked them. For one thing it kept everyone off her horse. After she got them bucking not quite so enthusiastically, I would sneak them away. She would get really mad at me, but I didn't care cause she only yelled at me and didn't ever hit me. Those wild-hearted horses became the best trail horses. Always sure footed on rocky trails and river crossings. Father had a herd of mustangs brought up from the Pryor Mountains of Wyoming. They caught a small herd of them and ran them through the branding chutes and into covered trucks. They were of all ages from aged mares to baby foals. Even the herd stallion was brought along. Some of them had their babies after arriving. That was one bunch of very wild and very scared horses. Cowboys came along to work with the horses and break them to saddle. The cowboys only stayed a short while. I think there were about twenty horses in the bunch. Twelve-foot high pens had been built to hold those mustangs. The pens had to be very strong, as the mustangs would slam themselves into them at the sight of anyone. Father may not have been a good house builder, but he knew how to build a strong pen. Father grew on the Wind River Reservation and had captured and broke wild horses to sell when he was a young man.

The horses were separated into smaller pens. A big snubbing post was set right in the middle of the big pen. The cowboys would rope a horse and snub it up to that post for haltering and saddling. Those horses would squeal like pigs when they were roped. Some of the horses would charge whoever was at the end of the rope and had to be roped with a second rope to keep them from killing anyone.

The herd stallion, which was called Poncho Vanilla, had to be sold to the rodeo, as he was just never going to tame and be useful for us. Also he kept the mares all riled up with his efforts to break them out.

All the colts and the old stallion were gelded when they were roped. This would help to give them a better attitude, and they would pay attention when being worked. When all the horses had been broke to halter and could be caught, they were turned out into the big pasture. It was now time to break them all to ride. Each day a few were caught and returned to the pen for that day's work. The cowboys would saddle and buck out each horse; then they'd ride them around the big pen until the horses understood what was wanted of them. After they came around to some understanding, the gate would be opened, and they were ridden in the open. It took a few times of riding before they'd quit bucking and started to respond to the reins. Some of those horses became our best saddle and packhorses, but there were a couple that just never were reliable. Therefore, they were unusable horses. Those were the ones Fay rode. Nobody else wanted to ride them, or they'd spend more time on the ground than in the saddle.

There was one very small horse named Crooked Creek. What a smart little horse he was. He was totally not rideable. Fay loved him the most. It got so she could ride him if she paid attention at all times. If for one moment she relaxed, he knew it and would go to hogging. Ironically, after he bucked her off, he would wait for her to get back on. It was a game they played. Crooked Creek was four or five years old when he came to us and about twenty-five or twenty-six when he was passed on to another family. He would still buck you off if he took a notion. What a cute little horse he was.

One of the best horses out of that mustang bunch was a brown mare with very large ears for a horse. She was named Banana Ears. She was a sweet tempered mare that anyone could ride. We had her for many years. She was great for any green rider, and you could pack anything on her, even bear hides, unlike another mare we had named Molly. Molly was round as a barrel and had short legs. Anyone could ride her, and she was a great packhorse unless she smelled bear. Then all hell broke loose. Molly would bellow like a bull and charge around kicking anything near her. She would kick trees, rocks, or anything in her way. On one of her rampages she kicked a poor hired hand in the face. He had to be taken to the hospital where they removed thirteen teeth and wired and pinned his mouth together top and bottom. He never worked for father again.

Stella got a pretty little sorrel mare named Dolly. Dolly wasn't very big, but she had a big motor and was an excellent mountain horse. The one bad thing about her was that no one could catch her except Stella, which made Stella happy because nobody could ride her horse. It made father swear a lot. Other than that Dolly was a wonderful little mare. There was another little horse Fay liked to ride. His name was Little Man. I would ride him whenever I could sneak him out. I begged father to give him to me, but he never would. Little Man was a fast horse, that's one reason I liked him. I'd run a horse everywhere I rode. The faster the horses could run, the more I liked it.

Running down our dirt road in the summer was a lot of fun if it was dry. There would be five or six inches of dust to kick up. We loved it. We would ride through the dust three or four times a day just to see how big of a dust cloud we could make. Of course, the person in front didn't have to choke on the dust. That's where Little Man came in handy. He was always in the lead. On one of our rides to the dusty area, we met a bear. It was a mother bear, and somehow we'd gotten between her and her cubs. She started popping her jaws and coming at us. We all ran, the horses running like never before. The last horse was a red and white pinto gelding named Apache. Johnny was riding him. Johnny looked like a squirrel sitting up there. Johnny had dropped his reins and grabbed hold of the saddle horn. He was kicking with both little bare feet and yelling at every stride "Go Patchy! Go!" I don't think Apache needed much encouragement, as he soon out distanced everybody. The bear went back to her cubs after a few feet, but we never stopped until we got home, which was a good four miles.

We had a lot of horses, but after father would take all he needed for hunters and pack trains, there sometimes weren't many left to ride. At least not many anyone wanted to ride. On one of those occasions, I was left with out a horse. I whined to one of the hired men about not having a horse. He told me he would get me a horse, and he did. He saddled it for me. Unfortunately, what he found was a wild horse named Satan. The man claimed he thought it was a horse named Blaze. Blaze was a nice horse, and father had taken him. Satan and Blaze did look nearly alike, but after that ride I had no problem telling them apart. After the man had saddled the horse for me, he kindly lifted me up in the saddle. Satan was off like a stone out of a sling, bucking at every jump. I hung on for quite a while. Well, it seemed like quite a while. Satan headed for the woods. I looked up to see he was heading right for a big, over-hanging limb, so I jumped. Well, I tried to jump. I had assistance from Satan that would have been okay, except Satan decided he hated me and would stomp me to death, which he proceeded to do. The hired hand ran to my rescue, hitting Satan in the head with a big stick. I was in pretty good shape except for a few broken fingers and a few cuts and scrapes. Mother put turpentine on the cuts and scrapes. She then straightened out my fingers and tied them to a small board for each hand so they would heal straight. Well, they healed fairly straight, with a little crooked, but not so bad. I didn't need a horse to ride for a couple of weeks after that. I hung around the house and whined and made everyone wait on me. I got as much mileage out of my slight injuries as possible. I tried to make everyone feel sorry for me, but only the hired hand did. When father returned from the mountains, he sold Satan to the rodeo for a bucking horse. That made everyone happy, including Satan, because now he could buck as hard as he wanted and be praised for it.

During the time my hands were healing, Johnny and I built a playhouse on the hill. We dragged boards up there and took a hammer and some nails. We used a tree for the side of the house. Johnny did all the hammering, as I couldn't hold a hammer with my hands yet. He nailed all the boards to the tree while I held them in place. Then we pulled up large sheets of moss to cover the house and hide it from sight so no one would find it. We spent a lot of time playing there on the hill, but after that summer we forgot about the playhouse.

Twenty-five years later, Johnny bought that piece of land. I stopped by to see the house he was building. Johnny ask me to take a walk with him saying, "Hilda, there is something I want you to see." He led me up the hill, not twenty yards from his new house. There was our playhouse. It was not as I remembered it. Not a big two-room playhouse. No, it was just two little piles of boards nailed to a large tree, and only about four feet high at the top. The rusty old hammer was still there. My heart swelled, and I came away with tears in my eyes. The memories of those times are sometimes hard to carry. It was such a time of closeness to family and nature that we will never have again. Many of the family and friends are now gone. Some of those friends were animals. They were a very large part of our lives. The dogs, horses, and other animals made it possible to live the life we did. Without them, we would have died of starvation, froze, or something terrible.

Mother chopping firewood

Standing left to right: Fay, Mother (pregnant) and Lucy.
Sitting from left to right: Bonnie, Johnny, Hilda and Stella

CHAPTER 7

I always thought mother was a big fat lady, but she was just pregnant all the time. Of course, I was a very small child myself. We have one tall sister in the family. She is five foot, four inches tall. Father was only about five foot five inches tall, but my brother, Johnny, reached six feet. I guess he got all the height genes. For some reason we always had some really tall horses. You pretty much had to stand them in a hole to get on or put a saddle on them. We had short horses as well. One in particular was named Shorty Horse. He was very fat, short, and slow. He even walked slow. He also had a mind of his own. If you wanted him to go left around a tree, he went right. When he came to water, even if it was only a foot wide and two inches deep, he wouldn't step in. You would have to fight with him to get him to cross that little creek. Then he would jump ten feet farther than was needed and about break your ribs on the saddle horn.

On a hot day in the summer I was riding Shorty Horse around the field where all the other children had been enlisted to pick sticks out of the new field. I had tonsillitis, so I didn't have to work. I just rode around and made fun of the other children because they did. They got pretty tired of me sticking out my tongue and smirking at them when mother wasn't looking. There was a neighbor boy working with them. He had a few firecrackers. While I was laughing at the girls, he went behind me and threw a firecracker under Shorty Horse. When that firecracker went off, so did Shorty Horse. He went straight up then lit out like it was the Kentucky Derby. I was on bare back and when Shorty Horse jumped, I fell under his neck. I was holding on with both my arms and legs wrapped around his neck. About a half mile later, he stopped. I was really glad to let go. No one had ever seen him run before that day or after either. I don't remember riding him again, although the whole event was really my fault for being a brat.

I wasn't the only brat in the family. I think we all had our moments. Lucy out did herself one particular time. We were playing hide and seek. Stella and Lucy decided to hide in the old converted bus. Lucy told Stella to hide in the icebox. Stella was really quite small, so she crawled right in. Lucy shut her in and went to hide herself. Well, the

Memories of an Alaskan Mountain Family

freezer door could not be opened from the inside. Lucy went on her merry way after being found, forgetting about Stella in the icebox. It was a really good thing there was a quarter inch drain hole in the bottom of the icebox. Stella pretty much stood on her head to get her face near that hole. A couple of hours later Fay was looking for Stella, and Lucy remembered where she had left her. Fay ran as fast as she could to get Stella out of the icebox. Stella was unconscious. When Fay opened the door, she tumbled out. After Stella got some fresh air, she woke up, no worse for the wear except she's afraid of small spaces now. Boy, was Fay mad at Lucy for doing such a dumb stunt.

The weather was hot and dry that summer. I think a lot of time was spent picking sticks out of that field. At least, it seemed like we picked sticks all summer. We not only picked sticks in our fields but the neighbors' fields as well. Father rewarded us with soda pop, which he put in the well to stay cold. The well was a wooden keg buried in a spring. When it was time to get the sodas out of the well, one of the bigger children would jump in the keg and hold onto the sides, grabbing the soda bottles with their feet. The little children couldn't get the soda out of the well by themselves, which probably saved a lot of soda. We tried to get at the soda, but the water was too deep. As summer progressed, the water got lower from lack of rain. Then we were able to get into the sodas, but that took both Johnny and I. One of us would jump in the well, grab a soda, and hand it up. Then the one up top would give a hand to help the other out of the well. We wanted out of the keg as fast as possible, as that spring water was freezing cold. Your legs would go numb by the time you got two sodas.

71

Small Moccasin Tracks

A lot of time was spent at the lake on the edge of our homestead. None of us could swim, but the lake was shallow for quite a ways out before it dropped off into the deep. We played in the water and pretended to swim. Really, we were just crawling along in the mud, making sand houses to put frogs in and catching little fish in our rusty old cans. The two kinds of fish we caught were sticklebacks and bullheads. Both have needle spines. You have to be careful not to get stuck, but getting stuck by those little fish was the least of our problems. The lake was and still is full of large black and green leaches. Some of those leaches are eight to ten inches long when they are stretched out swimming. We would pull thirty to forty leaches off our bodies each trip to the lake. They don't hurt when they get on you; they just make you bleed, and they are gross. After we pulled the leaches off, we would put them in cans and cover them with salt. It seemed to kill them, and we thought they needed punishment for biting us. We didn't like them, and they were useless to us because we couldn't eat them. The mud was great to play in. We spent so much time at the lake that father bought a big twenty-man survivor raft. It was big, round, and yellow. The hired hands anchored it on two sides to the shore and set it afloat. What fun we had with that raft. The older people used it to dive into the deep water, and the little people played on and around the shore side. We could even duck under and get out of the sun. There was a foot of air under it, although if you didn't watch out someone in the raft could step on your head. A fire pit was made by the water's edge. Many hot dogs and marshmallows were roasted there. Some life vests came with the raft. Us small guys used them to swim in the deeper water. We did learn to dog paddle after a while, but we stayed close enough to the shore to touch bottom when not wearing the life vests. I still am not a strong swimmer. Johnny was a worse swimmer than I was. He still swims like a rock to this day.

A lot of waterfowl nested at the lake. We caught a lot of baby ducks that summer. Probably the same ones were caught several times, as father made us turn them loose after we held them for a little while. Father was right. Those baby ducks and geese were better enjoyed swimming on the lake. Thankfully, we were allowed to catch as many frogs as we wanted, and we wanted to catch a lot. We brought buckets to put our frogs in. There were a lot of frogs and pollywogs in the lake. Some frogs still had tails, not being fully changed from pollywogs. Sometimes, we would take a few frogs home in the buckets. We would always turn them loose after a while. We could easily get more.

There was an old man that lived on the opposite end of the lake. He never wanted us to play in the lake. He got his water out of the lake and thought we were making the water dirty. I guess he never noticed the birds and muskrats that lived there, or the horse that fell through the ice in the winter and drowned. It never came out till spring when it finally went aground on the shore. Everyone called the old man The Crazy Fin. He was crazy, and he came from Finland. He really wasn't that crazy, but did have some strange ideas. He also made a lot of wine. Maybe he drank a lot of it, which made him a bit crazy. He also made a lot of nice boats that he sold. Some times we would climb in his boats. He never liked that and would yell at us in Finish and shake sticks at us. We couldn't understand the words but were pretty sure of what that stick shaking was all about.

Small Moccasin Tracks

One day when we were playing at our end of the lake. The Crazy Fin came sneaking through the woods behind us. He came out and surprised us waving a stick. We ran, but my little sister was only two years old and didn't get away. He hit her and broke her little arm. After that, Father had enough of Crazy Fin. He went to see that old man and was very angry. After that father's visit, the old man was nice to us. He brought us some boxes of concord grapes. The first grapes we had ever tasted. Mother gave us some to eat but saved most of them to make jam. I liked them better as grapes. Crazy Fin had a strawberry patch too. His strawberries were really big and sweet. We would raid his patch sometimes when he wasn't around. That is until we saw how he fertilized them. We would all hide and spy on him at times. The big girls were watching one day. They saw him using a bucket with the bottom cut out for a toilet. He would dig a hole in his garden then sit on that bucket bare bottomed and fill it. We never stole another strawberry from him. Whenever he brought mother any vegetables after that, she fed them to the livestock. That Crazy Fin was a little crazy after all.

Johnny and I made friends with the old man and brought him squirrels and sometimes grouse. He would tell us stories about his home in Finland, and sometimes he would give us lemon drops. He told us about those bad kids on the other side of the lake. Telling us to stay away from them, because they were always in trouble. I don't know where he thought we came from, and we never told him. Johnny and I got along with him quite well. We enjoyed his stories, and he enjoyed the squirrels and grouse we brought him. The little friendship worked for all of us.

74

Memories of an Alaskan Mountain Family

We found many ways to entertain ourselves, making fun from whatever we did. We never knew we were poor, because we had horses and dogs and as much freedom as anybody could have. There were times when we were hungry, but we always had fun. When we took the horses to camp in the mountains, we never brought food with us. We were sure to find something to cook. We would catch fish and stuff them with berries or mushrooms. Then we'd put them on a rock on the edge of the fire to cook. We would cook porcupine on sticks in the fire or wrap the meat in big leaves to cook under the coals. We ate berries and mushrooms by themselves, and in the spring there were always fiddle head ferns to eat. Those are really good, raw or cooked. Of course squirrels and grouse cook over the fire too. If we got really hungry, we could always saddle up and go home.

On one of those trips, Fay found a baby porcupine. Fay decided to keep it for a pet. She carried it home in her shirt. The baby was so soft, but it had tiny quills, which she didn't feel working their way into her tummy. When she pulled the baby from her shirt, her whole stomach was covered in tiny quills. Father and mother worked for a couple of hours pulling all of those tiny quills out of Fay's stomach. You have to get them all out, or they will work their way in farther and can even cause death. Fay's stomach was swollen for quite a while after that. She kept that baby porcupine for only a couple of days. Then one morning, it was gone. It had chewed its way out of the wooden box she'd kept it.

Lucy on the other hand had a pet mink and a magpie. Her magpie talked a little. When it got excited it would scream, "Pete! Pete!" Pete was his name. After Lucy left to get married, Pete went back to the wild. He would come back every now and again to visit, checking in and looking for a handout. He would fly down and yell, "Pete! Pete!" Stella found a baby muskrat under the woodpile and kept him for a pet. His name was Henry, and we had him for a long time. Henry liked to climb into people's laps and be fed a treat. If you never gave him anything, he would bite you. He didn't bite us to hard, but he bit strangers. He really didn't like strangers anyway. Henry's teeth were long and sharp, and a person could get a deep and nasty bite. If we didn't like a person, we wouldn't warn him not to pet Henry. Henry only let us pet him, but if he were in a bad mood, he would bite us too. He could be a real sweet pet and roll over to have his belly scratched. He liked to sleep with everyone, on the pillows. He chewed up a lot of stuff in the house. Once he chewed a hole in Fay's clothes' chest and chewed up her new jeans. Henry also bit through an electric cord and burned his mouth. He healed up and never quit chewing up everything. I think Henry went back to live in the wild after a couple of years. We really loved having him in our family. At least father told us Henry went back to the wild. I hope he did and had a family there. We had many wild animals share our lives through the years, even a baby bear, but that never worked very well. The baby bear slapped at little sister Bonnie. Mother slapped the bear, and the bear slapped mother. Bonnie was not scratched. The bear was not hurt, but mother had to have her arm stitched from wrist to elbow. Her arm looked like a zipper after that. I think they let the bear go back to the woods to find his mother. After all, he was a baby bear. It seemed we liked all animals, and a lot of them liked us. Our dogs and horses were always with us throughout our childhood and beyond.

Memories of an Alaskan Mountain Family

In winter father would get cull potatoes from the farmers for horse feed. They were just dumped on the ground and would freeze solid. They were great feed and kept the horses fat during the cold weather. As the potatoes were frozen, they made great throwing stones, which brings me to the Great Potato Fight. Father always took in homeless people in the winter. They were grateful for a warm bed and dinner, and father had someone to help cut wood and whatever else needed doing when he wasn't home. That's how a man named Bill Applegate came to spend the winter with us. He would entertain us with stories of his life on the Toadasack River. Now, I don't know where this river is. It may have only existed in Bill's mind, but according to Bill, a large amount of very big dumb bears lived there. I only say they were dumb, because Bill told us that he had outsmarted them on several occasions. Having been around him for a while and seeing some of the decisions Bill made, those bears couldn't have been that smart. The more wine Bill had to drink, the more exciting the stories became. One day while mother was baking bread, she had Bill entertain us with his stories. Well, Johnny got tired of listening to Bill and started throwing a ball into the wall. Mother yelled at him to stop throwing things in the house. Bill at that moment got one of his less than brilliant ideas. He got up and asked Johnny if he wanted to throw things, why not go outside and have a potato fight? Bill was unaware of what a colossal mistake that was. Johnny ran for the door, not even stopping for a coat. I guess he knew he wouldn't be outside long. On his way past the frozen potato pile, he loaded up on ammunition.

There was a pile of snow not more than ten or twelve feet from the door. It was snow that had been shoveled from the path and steps. Johnny ran behind that snow bank and laid out his ammunition in a nice orderly row. Bill never had a chance. When Bill stepped out that door, he was machine-gunned down. Johnny's little arms were spinning like Gatling guns. Bill took the first potato right between the eyes. I think he must have been hit two or three times on the way down. After Bill went down, mother and the older girls dragged him into the house. He was out cold and bleeding. There were several goose-egg size lumps rising on his head. Now, I don't know if one of those potato missiles knocked him out, or if it happened when his head came in contact with the ice on the path. Either way he was unconscious and bleeding all over the path when the potatoes quit flying. Johnny at the age of seven was declared the undefeated potato champ. Of course, he went unchallenged because nobody else had a death wish, which brings me back to how smart those bears really were.

Hilda in the snow. Fay fully dressed. Dogsled full of water cans

CHAPTER 8

Our dogs were lifesavers for us. They were used for so many jobs. They could really pull a heavy load. The rivers were our winter highways. All the supplies and even the logs to build cabins were freighted up the river ice. In the summer, the dogs were packed to go places the horses couldn't. The dogs were also kept in camps to keep bears away. Many a person was saved from hypothermia by having a dog to keep them warm at night.

Father always had a small dog that went with him everywhere. He called his little dogs his sleeping bag warmers. The first small dogs he owned that I can remember were Cocker Spaniels. Later, he always had a Pomeranian. The Cockers were always named Cody. The Cockers were good little hunters, and some of them would retrieve birds and other small game. There may have been four Codys. The Pomeranians were good little dogs as well. They would ride in the sled or father had a bag rigged on the saddle horn for the dogs when he rode a horse. The little dogs were trained to jump up, and father would catch them place them in the bag. There was a hole near the top of the bag for the little dogs to look out. I think those little dogs really liked to ride on the horses. When father was sleeping, no one wanted to go near his sleeping bag, as the little dogs would come out biting. No one cold just pick up father's coat or hat either. We thought that was funny and would tease the little dogs. We'd pretend to grab at father's stuff just to get the dogs upset. Only strangers would actually get bit. All the little dogs chased squirrels. If they ever caught the squirrels on the ground, they would kill them. The Cockers would climb the lower branches of trees after squirrels. One of the smartest little dogs that lived with us was a Schnauzer named Suka. She was Lucy's dog. Suka was a great little retriever. She would even dive into the lake and get stones you threw in. Well, she'd not always the stone you threw, but she always came back with a stone. She also was a good squirrel dog.

Fay had a big Border collie named Mike. Mike pulled Fay on the hand sled to school when we lived in Chickaloon. He looked just like Lassie. You could always tell when Fay was coming, as Mike barked continuously even if he was just following her, he barked. He fought with all the sled dogs, all the time. Also he bred father's sled dogs, and we got half Collie puppies. They all pulled real well. Most barked just like Mike. Mike did not like porcupines. He tried to kill every one he could find. Fay spent a lot of time pulling quills from his face. Mike would always get between us and anything he thought was dangerous, even bears. He would walk the little kids to the outhouse at night. The moose would come in our yard at night to look for vegetable snacks, but we were safe with Mike at our side. He was one of the few dogs that ever took baths at our house. Fay bathed him and combed his hair regularly. She loved that dog.

I had a little white sled dog named Snooks. She was kind of a runt, but big enough to pull me on the hand sled. She was actually quite fast. The only trouble was that she would chase moose. Sometimes on the way to school, she would see a moose then it was all over as far as school was concerned. She would leave the trail and go after the moose. You might as well roll off the sled, because you'd wind up in the woods anyways. After the moose ran away, Snooks would be back to work. There were quite a few times when I was late for school because of moose trouble. Sometimes the sled would get caught in the woods, and I had to follow her barking to find her and untangle the sled. There were times that I never made it to school at all, which was okay with me. I would rather play in the woods anyway.

Although if I didn't show up for school after a reasonable amount of time, one of the older girls were sent to find me. Usually Fay was sent, as she was the best tracker in the bunch. I would much rather Fay found me. She never was mean about anything. Lucy, on the other hand, thought it was her job to take a switch to me. It really hurts to get switched when you are cold. I think Lucy was a little more enthusiastic than was called for when it came to the switching too. Lucy would always drag me back to school. Fay would let me go home most of the time. Of course, Fay would give me a good talking to first. Fay always had the softest heart for us little children, and we knew how to use that to our benefit. Oh, she knew what we were doing, but she just would smile and pretend we got away with something. She was our little mother. Fay would make sure all the children had something to eat, even if she didn't eat. She made many sacrifices for us. She would even give the little ones her hat and mittens if they were cold. Oh, she would admonish us for what we should have done, but never with malice. She is still of that same heart today. One of her favorite sayings even to this day is," lazy children make lazy adults."

Bonnie was the best dog handler of us all. If she couldn't get it done with the dogs nobody could. She was also a really good trapper. Bonnie made a little money trapping the area closer to home. She always used the money to help the family, using only a small part for herself. Father gave us all traps, and we were all schooled in the use of them. This helped everyone, as it kept the predators down around home. Mother didn't lose as many chickens after the big girls started trapping. Fay never liked trapping. She always would feel bad for the poor animals, but we had to live also. Johnny and I started trapping later with small traps and snares. We mostly caught rabbits and a few weasels. We also caught a lot of muskrats. When we got older we trapped bigger animals. The larger traps are hard to open for small children. We ate a lot of rabbits though, which we caught in our snares. Once Bonnie caught a beautiful lynx and was drying the hide by the stove. A spark flew out of the stove and landed on it. Poof! It was gone! That was a lot of money to go up in smoke. Even mother cried for her. Thankfully, Lucy caught a wolverine a few days later, and it made her feel better.

The fur buyer would come to our house a couple times during the trapping season. Father would haggle with him over prices. After a deal was made, they would laugh and enjoy a meal mother had cooked. Mother got to know fur quality quite well. She could haggle with the best of them. I think she sometimes got a better deal than father did. She would not back down on what she felt was fair. I saw the time when she just picked up all the furs saying she would just wait for the next buyer. She meant it. Well, that buyer knew it and caved in to the price mother wanted. Father would have taken what the fur trader had offered, but mother had gotten an extra hundred bucks. That was a lot of money back then.

Mother never did any skinning of furs, but did help with the stretching. Lucy and Bonnie became the best skinners and stretchers. They never made many mistakes in skinning. So they always had prime hides. They were both excellent shots as well. Lucy shot a black bear that had been getting into the food storage, when she was ten years old. Mother and father were quite proud of her. Mother always was happy to get bear fat to make lard. Father would make smoked hams from the bears and sometimes made sausage.

Bonnie was the most fearless of all the children when it came to hunting, trapping, and dogsledding. Bonnie would hook up more dogs on her sled than anyone. Sometimes, she had as many as fifteen dogs. Boy, could she fly down the trail. She would haul more on her freight sled than anyone as well. Her little body would lean far out to take the corners and keep the sled upright. Dogsledding is more than just hanging on. You work the sled by moving your weight around on the back runners, even squatting on one runner and leaning out as far as you can makes a big difference at times. Sometimes, you push with your feet while standing on a runner, and other times you do a lot of running behind the sled holding on to the handlebar. Freight sleds have no handle, just a gee pole. You use that while running behind to shift the sled around corners and obstacles. When you go down steep hills, you chain up. Wrapping chains around the runners helps the sled to go slower. Otherwise, you will find yourselves wrapped around a tree at the bottom of the hill, or you might accidentally run over your dogs and injure them. Either way, it's not a good thing. Father sent me to check traps up the Kings River. I took a friend with me just to have company. Father told me to be sure to put the chains on when I went down the hill on to the ice. I never did it. I thought between my friend and me, we could hold the sled back. Sure enough we couldn't. That sled hit a tree at the bottom of the hill and smashed the whole front of the sled, and that was not the half of it. The towrope broke when the dogs hit the end of the rope. Off they went home. We had to walk about eight miles home and explain to father what had happened. Father never said a word about it. I think he was too mad. It was his brand new sled. I sure was nervous for quite a while. Father sent me again, and I did everything he told me to do down to the letter. I think if I had not listened a second time, he would have given me more than the silent treatment. I think I actually learned something from the whole experience.

Memories of an Alaskan Mountain Family

When Bonnie was around three or four years old, she was sitting in the sled father was getting ready to use. He had hooked all the dogs on but had not anchored it. For some reason, the dogs took off with Bonnie in the sled and no driver. The dogs ran under a barbwire fence dragging the sled with Bonnie inside under the fence with them. Bonnie got caught on the fence and her face was cut all the way to the cheekbone. Mother wrapped her face with cotton flour sheets and put grease on the cut itself. It healed, but Bonnie always had a scar across her cheek. Father always made a point to anchor the sled after that. He made sure we did also. Little things done or not done can have serious side effects.

Father never learned to drive a car. He would run a dog team or use horses whenever he had to go somewhere. He drove a dog team down the frozen Matanuska River to town in winter. In summer, he would use horses and go down the highway. Sometimes, he would pay a neighbor to take him to town in a car. Finally, he decided to buy a car and a truck for the hired men to drive him wherever he needed to go. That was a better idea. Things went a lot easier after that for getting supplies. Father even bought a truck to haul the horses around. We could then take the dogs or horses to far off places to hunt or trap, which made it easier to get our winter caribou. We just had to drive a hundred miles up to the Richardson Highway and shoot the caribou as they crossed the road. The caribou would be gutted and thrown into the truck whole to be butchered at home. Sometimes, we would leave them whole and let them freeze. We would just chop off whatever part we wanted to eat later. That worked really good as the meat never got dried out that way.

Small Moccasin Tracks

Father got one of his best female dogs by saving her life. One day a team of dogs showed up on our doorstep with no driver. Father stretched the team and anchored the sled then waited. A short time later, a man came walking up to the house. He was very angry and started beating the dogs. Father asked him to stop, but instead the man grabbed the little lead dog and started to break her leg over his knee. Father grabbed the man by the collar of his coat and told him if he hurt that dog anymore he would shoot him. The man was yelling about how lead dog was worthless, and he didn't want it anymore. Father just reached over and unharnessed her and told him to leave and never come back. Well, we never did see that man again. That little dog turned out to be a jewel. Her name was Trixie. She was a little shy, but I am sure that was because that man had treated her so badly. She was a great little lead dog. She really wanted to please whoever was driving her. Later, she produced some of our best sled dogs. Mother took a fancy to Trixie and she to mother. Mother let her run loose, as she never even looked twice at the chickens. Trixie followed mother everywhere. She was even allowed to sleep in the house. She would sleep with one of the children, keeping them nice and toasty on cold nights. Nobody minded that Trixie never smelled that nice. The babies always climbed all over her, and she loved them all. I don't know why that man didn't like her, shame on him.

All the lead dogs were special. They knew it. They were always showered with praise for doing a good job. Sometimes they were reprimanded for doing wrong, but not often, as they wanted to do it right. The way you punish a lead dog is by putting them on as a wheel dog. That really bruises their egos. Lead dogs think they are better than the other dogs. They look pretty pitiful when they are on the wheel. But when you put them back in the lead, they really try to please you. A good lead dog is worth its weight in gold. That little Trixie was a good lead dog. She never went on the wheel. The only thing bad about her was she was small. Sometimes she wasn't strong enough to pull all the dogs straight. We usually used her as a double leader. That way she had help. She helped train most of our lead dogs for quite a few years. When she got too old to work on the sled, she became just a housedog. Everyone always loved her. Every now and then, we would hook her up and let her pull the babies around the yard. That made both the dog and the babies happy. She was sorely missed when she went to lead that dog team in the sky.

In the winter of my eleventh year, we lived in a little house next to the old railroad bridge in Chickaloon. We only had to walk a mile to catch the bus. Some days, we didn't feel like going to school. On one particular day we were walking across the bridge when a young bull moose walked onto the road on the far side of the bridge. We started grunting at him to make him mad. We had done this before, and he would guard the end of the bridge thus preventing us from going to catch the bus. It was a good idea that had worked several times. The moose would not walk over the railway trestle on the planks, or so we thought. This time though was different, that young moose started right over the bridge. We of course ran back home, but the moose followed us right to the door.

My sister Bonnie had a boyfriend staying there with us. He was from New Hampshire and not familiar with moose. He thought he would go out and chase it away. We all told him not to try, but out he went anyway. That moose came after him, and he ran back for the door. Bonnie was holding the door and just before Chuck got there, she shut it. She was afraid the moose would come in also. Chuck ran for the side door and Bonnie beat him there and shut that one also. Chuck made two or three laps around the house before Bonnie let him in. The moose then ran away and started to strike a pony with his feet. Well, it was all well and good fun for the moose to chase Chuck, but when it started on the pony, father stepped out and shot him. It was out of season, so we just opened a shed that was right there, and everybody helped pull him in. We had fresh meat and so did the dogs. The other bonus was we didn't go to school that day. Although father knew what we had done and after he had a talk with us, we never did that again. We didn't want to get run over and stomped.

Our little house in Chickaloon had two bedrooms and a back porch. The back porch had been enclosed to make more sleeping room. Father and mother slept in one room, and the rest of us divided up around the house. Some were in the other bedroom. Some were on the porch, and the rest stayed in the small living room. The bedroom where the children slept had a full-length mirror on the back of the door. In the middle of one night, we were all awakened by Johnny screaming. He had gotten up to go out to the outhouse, and there was just enough moon to light a reflection in that mirror. He thought he was seeing a ghost, but it was just Johnny in a white T-shirt reflected in the mirror. It took a while for him to live down his embarrassment.

One year, the donation barrel had all sizes of ice skates in it. We all got skates. We had so much fun on the ice. Everyone helped shovel snow off the ice on the lake.

Memories of an Alaskan Mountain Family

For most of that winter that's where you would find us when we had free time. All of the children took to skates like ducks to water. The older girls built a big fire on the shore that way if we got cold, we could warm up and keep skating. The neighboring farms would let their children come skating with us. Sometimes, the neighboring parents came to skate with us too. They always brought marshmallows or hot dogs to cook on our fire. One lady brought hot cocoa that was a real treat that we didn't see often. Mother would come and watch sometimes. It was nice there by the fire. Mother always brought blankets for the little ones. If we skated late, they would fall asleep by the fire and be pulled home on the small hand sled. It was a wonderful time skating there on the lake under all those stars. It kept us busy, and we always looked forward to when we could skate again. Stella and I were about the same size, although she is one and a half years older. We skated together a lot. Sometimes if the wind was blowing, you could hold out you coat and sail on the ice.

We even went on the river to sail skate. The only problem being that as far as the wind took you downstream, you had to push into it skating back upstream. It was kind of hard at times, and very, very cold. Once when we were at Old Matanuska, Stella and I decided to skate the five miles down the Matanuska slough to the duck shack. Then we would ride a horse back. We forgot to take boots along to ride back with, and by the time we got to the duck shack, it was dark and cold. We didn't have boots and our feet were cold. We found some burlap feed bags and wrapped them around our feet and started the ride back. The weather turned for the worse. The wind started to blow and a snowstorm came up. The snow was a type of fine ice crystals that cut into your face. We burrowed our faces into our scarves, but they just covered with ice, and we had to stick our noses out to breath. It was a very cold trip. Maybe if we had walked it would have been better, at least our feet would have been moving. As it was, by the time we got back to Old Matanuska, our feet were almost frozen. Mother warmed our feet in lukewarm water, so as not to do more damage. Our feet turned black, and we lost quite a lot of skin. Our noses were frost bitten also, but not as bad as our feet. Thank the Lord that was all. It could have been much worse. We stayed off our feet for a few days and healed up well. We never forgot our boots again though.

The only time I got colder than that trip was when I went on the trap line with father. We went up the Chickaloon River to check thirty miles of traps. The weather was horrible. It was close to fifty below zero, and the wind was blowing hard. I was already cold and mostly just riding the runners huddled in my parka. I would run every now and then just to get my blood flowing. We were crossing small ice bridges over the river, going from side to side trying to stay off the big rocks. Father was running in front breaking trail.

We each carried our own gear and an extra sleeping bag. That way even if one sled got wet, we would have the same stuff on the other sled. We were about a half-mile from any shelter when the ice broke under my sled. I went in and held onto the sled so as not to go under the ice. I yelled at the dogs to get them to pull harder. It was not easy with half the dogs swimming in the river. I worked my way around to the front and pulled myself up onto the ice by holding the towline. I pulled with the dogs, helping them out

Father and dog sled on river freighting with lead dog, Tanner, running loose

of the river, and then we all pulled the sled out. Father had not stopped. He just headed for some spruce trees about a half-mile away. The sled froze up immediately, becoming a huge block of ice that didn't pull very well. My clothes froze on me. It was like wearing a suit of armor. I got behind the sled and pushed to help the dogs move the sled. It was hard work and took us awhile, but we made it to where father had started a fire and unloaded his sled to make a shelter. Father helped get the dogs and sled close to the fire so they could thaw out. I thought father had been mean to leave me there to get out by myself. But he did the best thing to save both our lives.

By the time I got to the fire, my hands were hard, and I couldn't move my fingers. If father had stopped to help me, we both would have died, because we both would have been wet and unable to strike a match to make a fire. As it worked out, we were both fine and were warm and dry soon. By "soon," I meant after my clothes thawed enough to get them off and get in a sleeping bag. Father's little dog crawled down into the bottom of the sleeping bag to warm my feet. Father got the dogs thawed enough to get off the harnesses and tied them up under some spruce trees where they could burrow under the needles.

We stayed there a couple of days thawing and drying out my sled contents. We shot a moose, so we had plenty of food for the dogs and us. The weather warmed up before we moved on, and the rest of the trip was not nearly as cold. We had a good load of fur on the trip back. Father sang most of the way home. He made up songs as we went along. It didn't take us so long to travel the thirty miles down the river and home. It was a happy homecoming. We could smell mother's freshly baked bread miles before we got there. All in all it was a great trip.

Hilda and Tubby at Old Matanuska

CHAPTER 9

Father moved us all to a house in Old Matanuska after he sold our homestead. We lived there for a few years. Father always found abandoned houses for us to live in. This place was on the edge of the Cook Inlet Tide Flats. Now the horses could be there year around. It was only eight or nine miles to the town of Palmer. The house had no plumbing, but it did have electric. There were four rooms and a back porch, plenty of room for our family. Lucy had married and moved away. Fay got married the first winter

93

there. She only moved to a small blue cabin a few hundred yards away. I don't know how big her cabin was, but it seemed to be about ten by twelve feet. She couldn't fit much in there and still have a woodstove to keep warm.

Johnny and I were happy, as we now had full-time friends. We met two boys that lived about a mile from us and a boy from town that spent a lot of time with us. Johnny and I would ride or walk up to Sam and Steve's house. We spent a lot of time fishing with those two boys. They knew all the good spots to go. Sam was the best fisherman of us all. I think he had fishing magic. Our family lived on the salmon the four of us caught. We even fed the dogs salmon. We ate a lot of rabbits as well. Once we got a beaver from an old couple that trapped the slough. There was a lot of waterfowl in the spring and fall, and we ate some of them as well. I went down to shoot a duck one evening and crawled through the tall grass slowly until I was quite close. I lined up a couple of birds and shot with the 4-10 shotgun. I knocked down two ducks and broke the wing on a goose. I ran the goose down and grabbed the ducks and lit out for home. I forgot the gun in my excitement and had to go back for it. We had roast duck and goose for a couple of days. We all took turns getting the ducks. Only the children hunted, as it was not officially duck season, but we still wanted to eat. I met a game warden on the road one evening just after someone had left to get a duck. I was riding a horse, so I ran him as fast as I could to stop the duck hunting. I got there just in time, and the gun was hidden under a log till that game warden left.

Johnny and our other friend, Harry, were riding the Shetland ponies through the meadows when a flock of Sand Hill Cranes flew up all around them. Johnny tackled one, and Harry jumped off and helped him subdue it. They proudly brought it home for dinner. Everyone was spooked about eating a Sand Hill Crane, as those were protected birds. Johnny and Harry were little kids though and only thinking of dinner. We spent a lot of time at Harry's house in Palmer. He had the best mother. Everyone called her Buzzy. She worked at the bowling alley cooking. Whenever Johnny and I came into the bowling alley, she would make us French fries and sometimes hotdogs. We ate at Harry's house many times. If it was suppertime, Buzzy set us down with Harry and fed us. She was a very good cook. I think maybe sometimes it wasn't just Harry we came to see.

When we went to hunting camp, Harry went with us. We had a lot of fun and adventures together. At one of the hunting camps, father gave us a can of Little Bear tent patching and some canvas to patch one of the tents. We worked for a couple of hours patching the tent. When we finished, the Little Bear patching glue was put in a wooden pannier. Hours later after eating supper, we pulled some panniers close to the fire to sit on. We sat there and talked for a couple of hours. We had just gone to our sleeping bags when the glue blew up. It completely destroyed the pannier Harry had been sitting on not five minuets before. We never knew glue could explode like that.

Harry was a lot of fun and made us laugh with his comic stories. He also had very loose joints and could bend his joints in very absurd positions, which was very cool when you are a child. We were entranced. Johnny and I tried to bend our hands and feet like Harry did, but couldn't come close. Harry wasn't afraid to try anything we were doing. He rode logs down the river with us and would ride the bucking horses. He was a tough little guy. Any idea we came up with, Harry was game to go with us to try it. He was a true friend. Actually, I still see him every once in a while when I visit Alaska. Harry is still a good friend. He has grown a bit taller now, and I think his hair has become about as grey as mine too. After all, we are only one month a part in age.

I think it was in the fall of 1963 that father took Stella and went to the lower forty-eight. They traveled to the East Coast visiting New York to New Hampshire. After staying on the East Coast for quite a while, they went to Florida and drove up to Wyoming. They were gone for a long time. In fact, they didn't come back home for almost a year. We had no money, so Johnny got a job sweeping out the barbershop a couple days a week. I am pretty sure that the barber gave him the job to help mother, as he really didn't need the help. Both Johnny and I helped at two dairies for milk and meat. Whatever we got from our work, mother made something out of it. We even helped a neighbor butcher a beef and got the tongue and heart. That was really good of them to let us work for something. We were just twelve and thirteen, but we were good with butchering. We got a young heifer for working for another farmer. We wanted to keep it, but we didn't have the money to feed her. We needed the meat more too. We would get food from school again. Whatever other children didn't want, we would take home. Mother would make it into something for supper. We saved a lot of milk from school. It really was needed at home. The school principal lived just up the hill from us. He started to bring extra milk to mother after school.

On Good Friday in 1964 an earthquake hit Alaska. We were home in Old Matanuska. The walls started cracking, and mother had us all go out and sit in the yard on a blanket. As we were sitting in the yard, cracks were opening in the ground all around us. Trees split in half with loud cracks. The ground was rippling like water. We sat on that blanket on the ground in terror. We all held hands in case we fell into the ground we could be pulled back out. At least, that is what mother told us. The earthquake seemed to go on forever. Finally with one last jolt, it stopped. We were afraid to move for quite a few minuets. When we did get up and walk around, we couldn't find any dogs or horses. The house had sustained quite a lot of damage, but we could fix it up good enough to live in. The road to town was destroyed and had to be fixed too. A neighbor told us to go up the hill, because a tidal wave was coming. We went up and waited on the hill. The wave never got as far as our house, but drowned most of our horses. Thirty-six horses were killed. Johnny and I went out to find the rest of the horses. We only found twenty. We brought them back near home, because the tide flats had sunk down and was now mostly covered with seawater. When the horses were near enough for other people to see them, they took them. They thought father was never coming back and decided to steal whatever they could. The dogs all turned up after a couple of days. Some farmers near town took our sled dogs so they could race them, but they never brought them back. We were really having a hard time feeding ourselves anyway, so I guess that was for the best.

Mother got tired of waiting for father to come home. She walked to town and got a job cleaning the lady judge's chambers. Soon the judge found us a small house on the edge of town. It was a nice little house with inside pluming and electric lights. It had a little dirt cellar. Johnny and I snuck out at night and stole a couple of our dogs back and kept them in that cellar during the day. After a while the farmers forgot about the dogs, and they were able to live upstairs with us. After we left the house in Old Matanuska, the neighbors stole all our things from there, even our big table that we had eaten at for so many years. I guess that's the way of the world. So be it.

Things got a little better after we moved to town, but Johnny and I worried about our horses. We had hidden a couple of them where nobody looked for them. We went back out there and got those two. Then we got ropes and waited until the middle of the night and sneaked into the barns and stole our horses back. We would walk them on rocks and in water to hide the tracks. The white men that had taken them weren't very good tracker, so we didn't have to work to hard to hide our tracks. If it had been Fay tracking us, she would have found us. Then we hid the horses in the hills where they could graze until we came back for them. We did this for several days until we had collected most of the remaining twenty horses. Then mother packed us some food, and we high tailed it out of that area during the night, taking all the horses with us. We took them thirty-five miles up into the Chickaloon Valley. Johnny and I took turns staying with the horses. One would go home to stay for a week, and then we would change. We only had the dogs and horses to keep us company during those weeks. I had a dog named, Izzy. She was the smartest dog I have ever known. She would catch rabbits, and I would cook them over a fire so we both could eat. She kept the bears away too. It was scary up there all alone. If we saw any people, we would hide. We couldn't let anyone know we were there. We were waiting for father to come back. He would need those horses when he got back. That was how he made a living. We waited all summer.

In the fall, Johnny started taking hunters after moose and caribou, even a few after sheep and bear. He was really making pretty good money, enough to support the family through the winter. Then father came home. Father took the horses and the rest of Johnny's hunters. Father finished out the hunting season. I don't remember him thanking us for saving the horses. Although he was glad to get the dogs back, he did say that. We never recovered very many dogs, only seven. It was enough to start.

Father had brought a new family back with him when he came. I guess he forgot about us, him being gone so long. The new woman didn't like us and had father get rid of us. So we stayed in town most of the time. Well, that new woman didn't have the strength that mother did and left father for another man that had more money. We moved back to Chickaloon with father. Johnny and I helped father trap that winter. Bonnie got married after she made it half way through the sixth grade. She was in the same class as me, but she was sixteen. So our family was getting smaller. Stella stayed with friends most of the time. So only the four youngest children were left. Mother moved back with father in Chickaloon.

Lucy came and took my little sister to stay with her for a few days. My little sister was old enough to babysit at that time. I think she was ten years old. She actually was a very good babysitter. While Lucy went somewhere for the day, my younger sister would watch Lucy's two little girls, Cathy and Roxanne. The babies were one and a half and two and a half years old. Once during the time Lucy was gone, the house caught on fire. My little sister got both of Lucy's little girls out and went to a neighbor's house. The fire department was called, and the house saved with minor damage. The newspaper called my sister a hero, and she was pretty important for a while. She had acted correctly in an emergency.

Lucy moved after her house fire back to a nice little cabin in Chickaloon. Her husband had bought twenty acres there beside the Matanuska River. The cabin had an upstairs and a nice kitchen. Lucy really liked it. She had us over for dinner in her new house. She could drive and picked us up in her truck. That was a fun time for everyone, although I don't think Lucy was a very good cook yet. Dinner was a bit burnt, but nobody complained. She did make pretty good bread. I ate a lot of that.

That year father bought more horses from somewhere in Michigan. There were four Welsh ponies in the truck, one for each of us. Norma got a white mare with a black head. She named her Beauty, and what a beauty she was. My little sister got a brown gelding, named Buster Brown. Johnny got a black gelding he named Diamond, as he had a perfect white diamond on his forehead. I got a black and white gelding I named Bob. Beauty was good to ride, Buster Brown was to slow, Diamond was a good little pony, but Bob was a pistol. He kicked and bucked, just my style.

Bob was the best river horse. He never lost his footing, even when the water got so deep it ran through the saddle. Sometimes, we had to swim, but he did that very well also. Mother liked to ride my pony, Bob. She trusted him anywhere. Of course, that was after I had ridden most of the bucking out of him. Bob just liked to buck sometimes. You know, for the fun of it. Johnny and I would ride to Palmer and race our ponies. We made a dollar or two that way. Johnny and Bob won all the barrel racing and pole bending competitions. Man, that pony could run and turn fast. Those big horses didn't have a chance. Johnny stuck to that pony like he was part of him. He was an awfully good rider.

Hilda on her pony named Bob

After winning some money racing our horses, some times we would go see a movie at the Center Theater before riding home. That was really something. Harry would go with us most of the time. After the movie, we would go with Harry to the bowling alley or his house if his mother wasn't working. Either way, Buzzy would feed us before we started the ride home. Buzzy was good to everyone, but I think she took a special interest in Johnny and me. Of course Harry was our greatest friend. We had other friends as well, but most of them were embarrassed to be seen with us, because we were poor. Not Harry. If he seen us across the street, he would yell and wave. We were friends, and that was that.

Harry was in my class, and we helped each other with our studies. I think he was a better student than I was. My mind was not always on my studies. Mostly, I was thinking about horses and dogs, and what I was going to do at home. Harry would always get me back on track. He would keep telling me, we had to get the schoolwork done before we could worry about home stuff. He always got his homework done, not always with me. I copied his homework sometimes, which didn't work that well if we both had the same stuff wrong. In fact, I got in trouble for copying.

Father put some colts in the corral to wean from their mothers. He told me to stay out of the corral. As soon as he left, I got a rope and caught one of the colts. Harry sat on the fence and kept telling me I was going to get in trouble. Well, he was right. That colt ran past me and kicked me right in the face. He broke my nose and busted my lip. I wanted to cry, but Harry was there, and I had to act tough. I held it in and cowboyed up. When father came back a little later, Harry told him that I was hurt. After father found out, my backside was hurt also. Harry didn't get me in trouble on purpose. He was sorry. I was sorry too. Because after my nose healed, I had a deviated septum. Oh well, I can breathe out of one side. Well, that was only the first time I broke my nose. Later, another friend hit me with a baseball bat. I was standing too close behind him. I was the catcher. I was supposed to be catching the ball in my hand, not the bat in my face. I guess it was a misunderstanding. Oh well, my nose was looking better and better with no plastic surgery. I liked the looks of my nose better after it was broken.

I had front teeth I didn't like the looks of either. Johnny fixed them for me. We were fighting and I was trying to run over him with my horse. Johnny ran behind a tree. When I ran my horse around after him, he had picked up a big stick and hit my horse right in the head. I bailed off the horse and was going to run Johnny down and trounce him. Johnny ran into the oat field and just when I was going to catch him, he flung himself onto the ground and kicked me with both feet in the mouth. He knocked my teeth loose and broke the bones that supported my front teeth. I held my teeth with my tongue because they hurt if I didn't. When they healed, they were pushed back a bit. At least I didn't have any more buck teeth, and it didn't cost me a penny to fix. Those were not the only bones I ever broke, but they were the best breaks I ever had. Some of the others didn't heal as nice.

We used to go a couple of miles up to Fish Lake to play with a pontoon raft someone had made and left there. It was a lot of fun, and also we could fish there and catch some nice land locked silver salmon. Once we took a friend along. As we were walking to the lake, our friend whom was carrying a big machete was boasting how if a bear dared come near us he was going to chop it up. He was walking first, then Johnny, and I was walking behind. Something went crashing through the brush. That boy threw the machete and turned and ran. He knocked Johnny down and ran over him, then did the same to me. I was just getting up when Johnny knocked me back down and ran over me also. I sat up and out of the brush came a very small moose calf. I collected up the machete and walked out to the road where Johnny and our friend were sitting on a tree limb, so much for manly valor. I was sworn never to tell what had happened. As I am sure that boy was quite embarrassed, but the three of us had a good laugh. I figure after all these years he won't mind me telling the tale now.

Another time, I walked my little sister down our road looking for berries. We went about four miles from home to where I had seen some raspberries the day before. We found the berries just fine and began filling our buckets. It was a nice large patch with heavy-laden bushes. When we had our buckets about half full and were moving more toward the center of the patch, we were surprised with a large black bear standing up right in front of us. It had been sleeping there after filling up on berries. We dropped our buckets and ran. Well, I ran. My little sister just walked like she was in a trance. I stopped and went back for her. She was barely moving. I told her if she didn't run that bear would eat her. That did the trick. She stopped altogether, just froze solid. I didn't know what to do, so I picked her up and threw her over my shoulder. She was about the same weight as me, but I guess my adrenalin was up. I ran with her on my shoulder for about two miles. Then I couldn't carry her any more. My throat and lungs were hurting from breathing so hard. I stashed her in a tree and went home to get help. A hired hand drove back and got her. There was no sign of the bear. I think really it must have been just as startled as we were and probably ran the other way. Good thing because we sure could not have out run it, if it had wanted us for an afternoon snack.

There were a lot of bears in the area, and we had a lot of confrontations with them. They never hurt any of us, but many times we were scared half to death. I never liked bears and always gave them any part of the trail they wanted. I had been chased up more than one tree. I know black bears can climb pretty good but not grizzly bears though, which is a good thing for me. One time, father took me with him on a bear-hunting trip. He had one hunter. There was a moose kill that father had spotted while glassing the mountainside from our camp. He took the hunter up there that evening to watch the kill waiting for the bear to return. Bears will eventually return to their kill. They stayed up there all night, and no bear came. When they came back to camp that morning, they found me as high in a tree as I could get. The tent was destroyed. There were feathers everywhere from the sleeping bags that had been shredded. All the food was ruined and the cans bitten clean through.

After father had left that evening, and I was asleep in the tent. The bear had come into camp and started ripping up the tent. The tent was tied between two trees. I ran out the back and up the tree. I don't remember climbing that tree, but that is where I stayed all night while the bear destroyed everything below. The bear really didn't pay any attention to me up in that tree. He was having way too much fun spreading feathers over about half an acre. Father took me with them to the kill that night, and the bear did come back to the moose kill. That hunter took home a real trophy for his wall.

Stella with trophy a bear hide

From left to right: Hilda, Johnny, and Judy (dog)

CHAPTER 10

The days are long in Alaska's summers. In the middle of the summer, they are endless. It's hard to sleep with the sun standing so high. Many a quiet evening was spent at one of the lakes. Covered from head to toe in clothes just to keep the mosquitoes off. Sometimes we were fishing and sometimes just sitting on a log watching the muskrats and waterfowl doing what they do. The haunting cry of the speckled loon would send chills up your spine. The beautiful trumpet swans sailed like schooners across the water, trailed by their small dark young. The loons built islands of woven grasses anchored to the mud two or three feet below the water. These are their nesting platforms. They were far enough out in the water to discourage most predators. The parent loons use these platforms not only for nesting, but they keep the babies there when they are not swimming them around the lake. Many times, you can see the chicks riding on the parents' backs when they tire. Loons are fun to watch, as they dive and may surface fifty or more feet from where they went in. Guessing where they will come up was a game we played. We rarely had it right. The loons eat a lot of fish, and that is what they are doing under water.

Some summer days never seemed to end. We had to think up things to do to fill in all that daylight. Johnny and I would sometimes walk or ride five miles to the highway. There we would sit on the hill and watch for cars go pass. There were not many cars going past in those days. We would wait for hours at times. To fill in the time between cars, we sometimes would make rock pictures on the sand bars of the river. We hauled as big of rocks as we could carry and laid them out on the sand bars. I once with the help of my cousins made a horse head one hundred feet wide. Tourists would stop and take pictures of our artwork.

One evening as we were sitting on the hilltop waiting for cars, we started to roll rocks down and across the road. That was fun. We were fifty feet above the road. That being so much fun, we decided to scare the people in the cars by rolling rocks down in front of them. They wouldn't see us and would think it was just loose rocks falling. That was our childish logic. We rolled a small rock down in front of a car then lay down so no one could see us. The car swerved and drove on. Well, that worked fine and was fun. We waited for another car. After a while another car came by, and we rolled another rock but a little bigger one. That worked even better. What fun! After waiting for over an hour, we heard another car coming. We got a fairly large rock this time. We rolled it down just like the others, but with much different results. As it turned out, the car was our neighbor's teenage daughter and her boyfriend. They saw us and stopped the car. They ran us down and beat our butts good. They also gave us a lecture. We deserved it, and that ended our rock rolling game.

Now, we had to think up something new. We had seen a movie called The Swamp Fox. They had bandits that rode around and raided at night. We decided to ride around at night and call ourselves The Night Riders. We had a real big club consisting of Johnny, me, and two neighbor kids. The neighbor kids had to be home by ten, so mostly it was Johnny and I. Our night raids consisting of riding past people's houses as fast as we could and yell real loud. I think some of our neighbors must have complained, as father told us to stay away from people's houses at night so they could sleep. We did. Then we made posters with Night Riders written on them to nail to trees. I'm sure the neighbors had a good laugh, but it was all in fun.

When Father and Stella returned to Alaska, they brought me three snakes, two lizards, and a horned toad. They were the greatest pets. I had them for quite a while. Well, a couple of months anyway. One of them escaped. We looked for it for a week. Then it turned up on the road. Some people from Texas were living in a small cabin up the mountain from us. They were coming to our house when they saw my king snake on the road. Being really ignorant, they shot it and brought it on to our house claiming they had shot a swamp adder. I was very upset to say the least. There are no snakes in Alaska; only what people have for pets.

Well, Johnny and I decided the person who shot my pet should pay. We made wanted posters for the murderer of our good friend. We tortured those folks for most of the summer. We nailed our wanted dead or alive posters all around their house. Then the Night Riders ran our horses around their house part of each night. We also followed them any time they went in the woods. We put axle grease on their outhouse seat. Sometimes, we would sit on the hill behind their house and hoot like owls for half the night. We just made their lives very uncomfortable. They moved away after a while. I don't know if we had anything to do with their move or not, but I wouldn't be surprised. We were quite the little monsters.

I gave my other two snakes to the school later that fall. They had a good home there. The Night Riders disbanded after that year due to lack of interest. Anyway, father got Johnny a Honda fifty motorcycle, so it would have been just me riding around on horseback. Johnny would carry me around behind him on that little motorcycle. I did ride around by myself quite a bit too. I just liked to ride. I really didn't like to spend time with to many people, mostly just Johnny. If he was busy, it didn't bother me to be alone. I had my horse and my dog. We went a lot of places together. Sometimes, I would ride in the mountains for a couple of days only stopping to graze the horse or to find something to feed the dog. It was a wild freedom I have never experienced again.

Memories of an Alaskan Mountain Family

Once while riding alone down our road, I met my sister's boyfriend. He was looking for her. I never trusted men, so when he came to close to my horse and reached up to touch me. I hit him across his face with my quirt. Then I ran over him with my horse. Now, I don't know what he was planning on doing, but if he was going to shake hands, I am sorry. I never waited to find out. I don't think he ever came back to see my sister again. If he was a nice man, I am sorry about what I did, but I never was very friendly. The fact he didn't come back makes me think he wasn't a nice man.

Our family never did do a lot of hugging or stuff like that. We were taught not to cry and to be tough and self-sufficient. These were the most important traits a person could have. Strong people don't show weakness, but that didn't mean we didn't love each other. We did and still do. It's just that most of us are not overly cuddly. In fact, I may always have been a little standoffish, but only to outsiders. I don't think to many people wanted to be to close to me. I slept with the dogs and horses after all. I still love the smell of horses. It makes my heart beat a little faster when I'm near one.

Being alone when you have a bad horse wreck is not good though. Once, while the family was camped on the Caribou Creek, I had a bad wreck all by myself. How that came about was pure stupidity on my part. I was riding on the mountain above the camp when I saw a porcupine waddling along. It was minding its own business. I was riding Apache, who was not trained to rope off of, but I decided to rope the porcupine and drag it back to camp to cook. I got it roped and turned towards camp all right, but that's kind of where things fell apart. Apache saw that porcupine dragging behind and spooked. I tried to stop him, but only caused more trouble for us both. Because I was holding him back, he started to spin and got tangled in the rope with the porcupine. Then with his legs full of quills, he went crazy. I got the rope loose, but it was to late, as he just went wild and charged downhill. He jumped over a steep bank and just went head over heels. He landed on me, and then kept rolling. I couldn't move for quite sometime. Things could have been worse, but after Apache got back up, he came over where I was and stood there. After about half an hour, I could drag myself with my arms. I got hold of the stirrup and pulled myself up the saddle enough that Apache could pull me back to camp. It took a while and a few times of loosing my grip on the saddle to get back to camp. Apache got me back. When we got back father and mother carried me in a tent, where I stayed for a couple of days. They thought I might not walk again, but I really worked hard at it and made my legs work again. Father was real mad at me for being a fool. He was really worried about the quills in Apache's legs too. He had to throw Apache down and pull the quills out with pliers. Apparently he got all the quills out, and Apache was fine after the swelling went down. It took me longer to heal, but I was at fault and deserved no less. Thankfully, with a little time and work, I was back in the saddle, maybe a little wiser for the wear.

Apache's fall was not by far the only horse wreck nor the worst one. I think it would take a shorter time to list the bones not broken from dealing with horses than to list the horses themselves. Of course, it was never the horse's fault. As my father would always say, "You need to be smarter than the horse." If you are training a horse and it gets exciting, you are doing it wrong. I must have had quite a few times when I did it wrong, but that's how you learn. My father was a pretty good slack roper. He could catch horse or cow anyway he wanted. I never was that good. I just never tried that hard. Some of my sisters were pretty good though. One time while riding through the mountains during the caribou migration, father shook out a loop to catch a caribou. It so happened that a good-sized bull caribou had run into a little box canyon. Father held his horse in the mouth of the canyon and waited for the caribou to realize his mistake and come back out. When that caribou came back out, father caught it by its horns. I don't know what my father was thinking. When that caribou hit the end of that rope, he flew off his feet and then came back up just as fast. Boy was he mad! He tried to charge father's horse. Father was trying to get out of the way and get rid of that rope at the same time. After a few loops around each other, father finally got the rope loose, and the caribou saw open ground. As far as I know, that caribou still has father's rope.

That was not the only poorly thought out idea father ever had. I remember a time when we were all riding down the King River trail when an equally wild idea hit him. Apparently when he rode through some brush, a couple of black bears jumped up in front of him. Father grabbed his hat and leaned over his horse's neck and started hitting the bear and whooping it up. We were behind and came out of the bushes just in time to see father running behind those two bears yelling and swatting. What a sight! Lucky for him the bears were too surprised by his actions to stop and fight. Father told us never to do that, as you could get yourself in some pretty big trouble. I don't like bears and would never have thought of doing that anyway.

Although my sister, Fay, once tackled a full grown Dall sheep ram, she held it down by laying on its neck and sticking one horn into the ground. She held that ram and yelled until father came and helped her. She really couldn't let it go without help, as it could have seriously hurt her. That ram out weighed her by over a hundred pounds. She said she didn't know why she jumped on that ram. It just happened to be right below her when she topped the rock. Instinct took over her, and the next thing she knew, there she was with that ram's horn stuck in the ground. Sometimes things just happen that way. Boy did that gave everyone something to talk about for quite a while. I'm sure Fay thought about it quite a bit, as that really was quite scary. After all there was a cliff only a few feet from where she held that ram. They could have both went over, and it was a long way down.

Fay was the best of us in knife throwing. She was fast and accurate. Throwing knives was something we all did. We also threw hatchets and axes, even machetes. Fay proved that it didn't mater what you used. One day Fay and Johnny were walking back from an old campsite. They had picked up a few items left there. One of those items was a long and sharp serving fork. They had been checking old campsites for stored food to make something for dinner. On the way back, a young snowshoe hare jumped up in front of them. Before she even thought about it, Fay had thrown that fork and instantly killed the rabbit. Well, rabbit was dinner for everyone but Fay. It had made her sick, and she felt really bad for the rabbit. We were just glad to have rabbit stew.

Fay was a good and accurate rock thrower as well. She brought many a ptarmigan or spruce hen home for dinner with just her throwing skills. Fay even brought down a few squirrels from time to time. Those little parka squirrels are very tasty fried or stewed. Many times, they were all that kept our backbones from touching our bellybuttons. Not that the rest of us couldn't throw a rock. We could, and we did our share of hunting with whatever was at hand. Fay was just a little better at it than the rest of us. Fay didn't like bears and still don't. She always told us she didn't want to eat them, as you don't know whom they had eaten last. It could have been your horse or your neighbor. Anyway, bears are just scary.

Father had taken Fay with him up the Kings River to repair trails. On the way back, a grizzly sow and her two-year-old cubs confronted them. It was a narrow spot on the trail, and they couldn't get away from the bears. Father jumped off his horse, grabbing his gun on the way off. Fay jumped off her horse. Father yelled at her to run down the canyon wall and get across the river. He would hold off the bears so she could get away. She ran down the canyon yelling how she hated bears.

Father drilled buttonholes up the front of that sow when she charged him. She fell dead at his feet. Then the cubs charged, and both had to be shot. Luck was with father and Fay on that day, well a little luck and a lot of good shooting. Father said he was sorry he had to shoot the cubs, but what else could he do? Father skinned out all three bears while Fay sat there telling him how much she hated bears the whole time. I only know this as father told us what happened when they returned home loaded with bear meat and three hides. Fay never had a lot to say about it, but I am sure that didn't help her relationship with bears.

Bears were always on our minds when we went in the hills and mountains. They also would come right to our house and tear up whatever they could. Once when father was bringing supplies home, before we had a truck, father had someone leave the supplies at the end of the road while he went home to get a horse and wagon. When he returned to get the supplies, a black bear had gotten there first.

Johnny between two black bear

The bear had torn open a fifty-pound bag of flour, then sat down beside it and pounded on the bag spreading flour everywhere. The bear had quite a fun time. When father came back and yelled at him, he ran away, but there went our flour. Father had to send someone back to town for more. Father said that black bear looked more like a polar bear with all that flour. It must have been quite a sight.

Many of our camps were destroyed each year by bears. I guess they were curious and maybe also looking for a snack. We always had to bury or put our supplies high in a tree. Black bears can climb quite well, so putting them in a tree didn't always work. Squirrels would also get into anything left in the trees, chewing open the bags so the stuff inside could drop down for the bears. I guess they were helping each other out without knowing it.

A lot of times, a sled dog was left to guard the camp. That didn't always work either. Very often we would return only to spend a few hours pulling porcupine quills out of the poor dog. Porcupines were very abundant and very destructive. They would chew up anything that had salt in it, and anything that had been on a horse had salt on or in it. If a saddle was left or a pack pannier, it probably would be chewed up on our return. Therefore, anything left had to be pulled high into trees and hung on ropes. Porcupines couldn't get them that way, but we still had squirrels to worry about. That was where those small dogs came in handy. They cleared a lot of the squirrels away from our camps.

Wolverines were not the greatest around a camp either. They not only tore everything up for the fun of it, they also peed on everything. As part of the skunk family, wolverine urine was not a pleasant thing to smell. After a wolverine had been in camp, most everything had to be thrown away, and if it was your sleeping bag, that was not very funny. Of course, there were always the sweat and hair covered saddle blankets to sleep in. I didn't mind them, but others did. I kind of liked the smell of those saddle blankets. Maybe others didn't like the smell of me either after I had spent the night sleeping in those blankets, but who cared. Sleep is sleep. Maybe the horses liked me better, because I smelled like them. That couldn't be a bad thing. Could it?

We slept under spruce trees when we could, as they usually have a deep and soft bed of spruce needles. Father had a saddle horse that always hung around the camp. If father was sleeping out on the ground, the horse would eat around him, then push father over with his nose to check for grass under the sleeping bag.

Early one morning when father was still sleeping, he felt a nose pushing him over and thought it was Steel, his horse. Just opening the sleeping bag enough to put out an arm, he whacked the nose that was bothering him. Turns out, it was a grizzly bear. Father's whack on his nose sent it running to the edge of the trees. When that bear bellowed from the whack, father came out of that sleeping bag mighty fast. He grabbed his gun and shot a couple of rounds into the rocks below the bear to scare it off. It sent him on his way. I guess that bear thought at first he had found himself a nice sandwich, but he must not have been too hungry. At least it was not hungry enough to fight for his dinner, which was real lucky for father.

One particular camp was always being raided by a bear. Father decided to snare the bear and stop the vandalism. He anchored a snare to a large log in some bushes where the bear had been traveling through to reach the camp. A few days later father and mother went up to check on the progress of the snare. When they got to the camp, everything was in order except the log and snare were gone.

While father was looking for the snare and log, mother had to answer nature's call. She looked around and found a suitable big log to perch on. She was perched on that log when it began to move. Running with your pants around your ankles is not an easy task, but she was moving pretty fast in that condition. Father saw what had happened and was laughing so hard he couldn't stand. I can't believe mother knew all those names father said she called him as she was running and falling through the trees. She didn't deny she had called him everything she could think of, but she said he deserved every word. The bear did not want to catch mother. He had his own worries. No one got hurt except mother's pride, and I think she always checked a little more carefully around herself in the woods after that. Of course that ended the bear raids in that camp for a while.

Mother was not the only one to wind up in a similar situation, only it wasn't a bear the next time. A lady from town was at our house taking pictures when nature called for her. She ran behind a bush, pulled down her pants and squatted. About that time, a half dozen sled dog puppies' noses hit her butt. She screamed and tried to run not stopping to see what was attacking her. She flew out from behind the bush to land face down with her pants down around her ankles before all the other tourists and our family. Everyone was too shocked to do anything. Father quickly threw his coat over her and everyone turned around so she could get up and pull up her pants. Those tourist left right away after that. I don't think any of them ever came back. We had something new to tell the neighbors for a while anyway. Everyone had a good laugh, well, maybe not one lady.

Father on Klondike helping Killer (the dog) onto the saddle

CHAPTER 11

We had a nice camp on the Caribou Creek just on a bend in the river. A small creek tumbled down the mountain a few feet from camp. There was a framed tent there. It was pretty nice. Johnny and I would drag logs into Caribou Creek and ride them as far as the camp for firewood. There is no wood near the camp, and it was a lot of fun although the logs would have to dry out after the wild ride before we could burn them. Sometimes, we would drag the logs back to camp with one of the horses. Mother liked that dry wood better, but she never complained about the wood as long as we got some.

The Caribou Creek area is a good place to pan gold. Well, it was before a mining company dredged the whole river. When we were children, it had gold for the panning. Johnny and I panned for several days and got a little over an ounce. Thinking that someone would rob us, we decided to hide it. I have no idea today who could possible have been in those mountains to rob us, but hide the gold we did. Fifty years later, we still haven't found were we hid it.

While we were at that camp, we spent a lot of time riding the mountains on both sides of the river. We also climbed the mountains to walk the draws looking for sheep horns. Sheep horns roll easily and always wash down into the draws when the snow melts in the spring. We would collect them to sell to carvers, and if they were nice and big we'd sell them to taxidermy shops. Johnny and I could get two or three hundred dollars worth of horns on some trips. All the horns and any gemstones we found were put in a pile for father to pack out and sell.

There was a small creek about a mile upstream that had good size fish in it. Johnny and I went there to fish one nice sunny day. We had crossed and were fishing the opposite bank and doing quite well I might add. We had a stringer of fifteen nice trout. We weren't paying attention to what was happening on the mountain behind us, just into those fish. Then down the mountain stream came a small wall of water. We were stranded on the wrong side of the creek. I guess it had been raining up there pretty hard. It was still sunny where we were, so we just started a fire and cooked some of those fish and spent the rest of the day looking for good thunder eggs. In a few hours, we were able to load our rocks and our fish and cross back to the camp side. We had been thinking we might have to spend the night on the other side and were happy it had not lasted too long. It wouldn't have been unusual to be stranded on one side or the other of a river. It had happened many times. You just had to wait for the water to go down or try to swim it. If you try to swim it, you had to be very careful not to get washed off your horse and drown.

Stella tried to swim her mare, Dolly, and foal across the King River. The foal drowned. Stella was heavy of heart for quite sometime after that. We have rolled whole pack trains of horses down a swollen river, losing some of them, not to mention the supplies they were carrying. It can happen in the blink of an eye. People drowned swimming horses across rivers almost every year. That information never stopped us from swimming rivers if we took a mind to. I guess we were knot heads, and very lucky.

While we were at the Caribou camp, we found a perfect ammonite fossil. It was about ten inches across and sitting on a two-foot tall stone pillar. It was in perfect condition. It was too heavy for Johnny and me to carry back to camp. We hid it in some rocks up above the creek so we could retrieve it later. We never did get it. We left camp and didn't go back for a couple of years. By then the gold dredges came through, and everything was destroyed. Nothing grew anywhere near the river any more. All the fish were gone. All the small streams had been ruined. It was really quite awful. I shed tears for all the natural life that was destroyed. Everything was gone because of gold. It was a hard lesson for us. The land took many years to repair itself, but it never was the same though.

Father had a five-acre home site on Caribou Creek. We had always spent a lot of time there in a small cabin left by gold miners at the turn of the century. Well, really the cabin had been rebuilt several times. It had burned a couple of times, and the dirt roof fell in at least once. My older sister, Fay, owns it now. She built a beautiful new cabin there, but when we were children, it was a little dirt-roofed cabin. We used it in winter for a base camp on the trap line. In the fall, it was a base camp for hunting sheep and caribou.

In the summer we just stayed there to gather gemstones from around the area and fished the streams. The cabin was small and most everyone slept under trees scattered around the cabin. Johnny and I always slept under a large spruce tree on a small island beside the camp. The island was only about fifty feet from everyone else. We had our own fire pit. We spent many hours talking and sharing our dreams for our future sitting by that fire. We cleared the large lower branches of the tree to make a ladder in case a bear came during the night. We never had to use it though. I think Johnny told me that someone had cut down our tree a few years ago. It was probably ready to retire anyway, but it kept us dry and safe for a lot of years. I think I will remember it as it always was.

Early one morning Johnny and I went to get the horses. You could see them from the camp. They were a half-mile down the river eating grass on a sand bar. We got to the horse and started back to camp with them. We were each leading a horse. The other horses were following. Then the horses started acting spooky, snorting and looking behind. At first we couldn't see anything. Then we saw a couple of wolves trailing us, staying back a good thirty feet. That was too close for us. We climbed on our horses and stampeded back to camp. Everyone ran out to see what was wrong. My older brother was there. He shot at the wolves but didn't hit them. He just wanted to run them off. They didn't come back that trip. Father said it was a couple of pups, and they were just lonely.

Just around a bend in the river was a small stream that ran back toward the mountain about two hundred feet to the bottom of a waterfall. The waterfall was about three hundred feet high. The pool at the bottom had some little golden-finned Dolly Varden trout. I have never seen that variety anywhere else. They never got much bigger than about nine inches. They were a very fat little fish and tasty. Father let us catch a few each trip, as they were so rare, and he wanted to preserve them. Of course after the dredging, they're all gone. They sure were nice little fish. I hope some survived somewhere. That particular creek was the best place to find fossils. We hauled many pounds of fossil rocks from there. Father even found a dinosaur bone. He donated it to the University of Alaska in Fairbanks. That fossil was the only one of its kind ever found in Alaska.

Father had a gold mining claim somewhere on the Caribou, but he never did much with it. He sold it to the gold dredgers and was sorry he did after he saw what they did to the whole of the river valley. They never gave him much anyway. They never dredged his old claim though, so I guess it all worked out. They couldn't get their dredges up to that area. It was pretty much the only area they didn't ruin. The dredges don't care about fossils, so those were all broken and crushed along with everything else. They have laws now to protect the land and animal habitat from destruction like that, which is a good thing. Sadly, se still have people that only care about what they can strip from the earth. I guess it is tunnel vision. They can't see the harm they are doing. Also many don't care. They think it won't touch them. They are wrong, even wild animals don't dirty their own homes. The earth is our home. We need to treat the earth with respect, but I digress. Even though things have changed on the Caribou, nature has repaired a lot of the damage.

While climbing above the camp, Johnny and I found where a sheep had been killed in a rockslide. It had happened many years before we found it. It was one of the largest sets of ram horns we had ever found. They couldn't be measured for a record book as the skull had been crushed, but it certainly had been the king of the mountains when he was alive. The horns were no good for carving, as they were crumbly and had been chewed on by a porcupine. We gave them to one of the hunters to take home and put on his fireplace mantle. I guess even sheep have to walk carefully in the mountains. On that same trip, we came upon a mountain meadow where a pack of wolves had killed close to forty ewes and lambs just for the fun of it. None had been eaten, just torn apart. Wolves just like to kill. I have seen them run a moose down and kill it, then run off to find something else to kill. That is their way. On a winter trap line, trip wolves came through our camp and killed two of our dogs that were tied on chains. They just ran through our camp and in seconds the dogs were dead. The wolves never even stopped. We never even had time to pick up a gun before it was over.

I have seen packs of wolves that numbered above thirty and once a pack with over forty wolves. It takes a lot of moose and caribou to feed that many. Wolves will work a river valley until they have cleaned out every moose or caribou in it. Then they move on. In one valley, I came upon a very odd thing. The snow was all packed down for over fifty feet. Right in the middle was a dead wolf. The pack had killed him, one of their own. Why? I don't know, but it was an awful battle. Maybe he had challenged the leader, or maybe it was the old leader. I couldn't tell as it was so torn apart. I guess they have their own rules.

One summer day while we were camped on the Caribou Creek, father, Johnny and my older brother, John Joe, went to look for the horses. They never took guns, as they were just going after the horses. They tracked the horses eight miles down the river to father's cabin. They stopped for lunch before bringing the horses back. As they were sitting on blocks of firewood eating cans of fruit, they looked up to see a grizzly charging straight at them. Father could see an axe sitting beside John Joe. John Joe could see an axe sitting beside father. They ran past each other to get the axes they saw. John Joe grabbed an axe and turned to face the bear. Father grabbed an axe and started to bang it on a large piece of metal roofing. When the bear heard that clanging, he skidded to a stop and turned tail and got out of there. Father and John Joe looked around but couldn't find Johnny. They heard a small squeak from the top of a very tall spruce tree. Yep, it was Johnny. Father says he doesn't know how Johnny got up that tree as the limbs were too close together, but he swears Johnny passed two squirrels on the way up. Thank goodness bears don't like the sound of metal on metal, or it might have been a little longer lunch break than planned. I mean lunch for the bear.

Johnny is crying because of the bears. Stella is holding Jack donkey

Johnny never did like bears that much, even as a baby, but having been chased by a few, it is no surprise. Johnny became one of the best bear guides in Alaska in adulthood. He knew a lot about them, having studied their habits growing up in the bush. He could avoid them, as did we all. Most of the girls never spent many years guiding after they grew up. That's not to say they didn't know more than most men about hunting and trapping. If it was ever necessary, they could live quite well in the wild. They wouldn't go hungry, and they would have warm fur coats. It's just that most of the girls chose to live a more civilized life, raising a family with modern conveniences is pretty nice you know. Things like hot running water and electric lights are a real bonus. Indoor pluming is a real hard thing not to have

127

nowadays. I don't think I want to go back to my childhood living anytime soon. Well, not in the winter anyway. It's still wonderful to take those summer pack trips into the mountains though.

As we got older, we spent more time with father because we were a help to him. We all took our turns on the trap line and pack trains. We also helped him with his hunters. We were all knowledgeable in the woods. All of us could pack a horse or run a freight sled. Of course, we were raised in that way. When there were dogs to work, Bonnie was always first in line. When there was tracking to do, Fay was there. When it was chasing game to hunters, we all did it, but if it was sheep to chase, it was most likely Johnny. Not to say the rest of us didn't help, it's just that Johnny was just a lot faster than anyone else.

Sheep are not that easy to chase around cliffs and slides, which can fall a thousand feet at times. I have run myself into some pretty scary places trying to herd sheep to hunters. Sometimes, I have had to rope myself out of places I ran into. In the heat of the chase, you can really get yourself into a pickle. My nephew was with me on one such occasion. We were on a very small ledge with our backs to the wall, trying to figure how to get off that cliff face. He said, "Hilda, tell me how we did this again after we promised we would be more careful last time?" You know, I had no idea, but by helping each other, we got off that cliff without father's help. That kind of stuff really does scare the stuffing out of you. It would make father mad at us for being so stupid if he knew about it. He'd be right; we really weren't paying attention to what we were doing. I eventually learned to check my surroundings at all times. That is something everyone needs to do every day, wherever they are.

Father never was one to give praise often. We all worked twice as hard to get him to say we did a good job, but it was rare. I have heard from other people that we did well, which actually made me happy to hear. Even though the praise didn't come straight from father, it was still nice. I guess father really did like us, even though I was never sure. Maybe he was proud of our outdoor skills, he never said. He apparently didn't want us to get to full of ourselves. We learned a lot of our life skills from father. For one thing, he always told us be a friend to everyone, even if they don't like you. He said it would drive them crazy. You know it's true. He also told us it's not the wild animals you have to fear. They are pretty predictable. It's the human animal you had to worry about; as you never know which way he would jump. That was also true. Father was very wise in the way of the world. He had lived a long time and saw a lot of things. He came into the world in the time of horse and buggy and left in a time of computers and rocket ships. It must have been hard to understand the way things had changed during his lifetime. I have trouble with it, and I have only lived a little over half as long as he did. I am glad he never had to witness terrorism on our own doorstep.

Horses, Jack the donkey, and a couple of freight sleds and dogs

CHAPTER 12

When I was thirteen years old, I wanted to see more than trees. I ran away and went to Anchorage. After meeting some kids my own age, I stayed with them for a few days. I don't remember their names today, but they took me to their house, and I babysat their younger siblings. I don't know where their mother was, but she was not at home during the week I was there. It was the first time I saw roaches. I turned on the light in the bathroom and went shrieking out of there. Those little kids I was watching laughed at me and showed me you just bang on the sink, and all the roaches ran away. I thought roaches were horrid. I never went in that bathroom at night the rest of the time I was there. I also stayed out of the kitchen, as it was also full of roaches at night too.

The children my age were never there much. A week after I arrived in Anchorage, the older boy of that family asked me if I wanted to ride his motorcycle. Well, of course I did. I rode around the block and was stopped by a policeman. Apparently, it was stolen, and I was riding it. I was taken to the jail and held there. Mother was notified. Father told them to leave me in jail, as it would teach me a lesson. I spent four days in jail scared half to death. Mother showed up for court. I sobbed during the whole proceeding. The judge made me tell whom I had given me the motorcycle. Then he told me if I were ever in his court again, he would send me to prison with murderers and thieves. I was terrified. I promised never to do anything wrong again and to go home and help my family. I was very relieved he sent me home. Years later, I met that judge. He told me he had a hard time keeping a straight face during my court appearance. He said he had been sure I was going to be good, as he had never seen anyone so scared in his courtroom. He had laid it on pretty heavy. He had talked to mother before I'd been brought in. She knew what was going to happen. Well, it did set me straight. I never ran away again. The big city wasn't that appealing after jail.

A few days after my return home, we all went on a pack trip up the Tolcina area. We stopped at the Tolcina Lodge to camp for the night. While we were there, we went to look at some horses the lodge owners had purchased. They had hired a horse trainer to train the horses they had bought. When we went back to the corrals to look them over, the trainer was trying to work with a horse. Apparently, this man had no idea how to train a horse. There was a beautiful black quarter horse stallion tied to a snubbing post as close as he could get him. The man had a whip and was beating that poor horse half to death. I think father about lost his mind. He grabbed that man by the front of his shirt and threw him into the fence. Father told him to get out of there right now. Out that man went. Father went into the lodge and told the owners what was going on in the corral. They had no idea. Father offered to buy the horses right then. The owner sold the horses to father, and we put them in the truck and left.

That black stallion was terrified of all men after that. Father gelded him and tried to tame him, but that horse had no trust. I was quite enamored with that beautiful horse. I spent hours in the corral with him. Soon he was looking for me and would nicker when he saw me. Father saw what was happening and gave him to me if I could train him. I spent many hours with that horse. I named him Thunder. I brought Thunder grass and oats every day. Soon he was eating out of my hand. One day I slid onto his back from the fence. He looked around quite surprised to where I had gone, but he never tried to get me off. I fed him some grass from my perch on his back. Every day after that, I climbed on his back. I used a war bridle I fashioned for him from some rope I found in the shed. A war bridle is only a rope tied onto the bottom jaw. I never had to lead him as he followed me everywhere I went in the corral. After he got used to the war bridle, I would get on him and pull his head to one side or the other and encourage him to walk. He soon got the idea, and I was riding him around the corral. A hired man came by and opened the gate and told me it was time to move outside the fence. Everything was fine until we walked out to the road. Thunder saw freedom and lit out of there like a bolt of lightning. Well, I stayed on. I had forgotten to teach him whoa. After about a mile, he slowed down to a walk. We worked on whoa for a while. That was something he never did really well. That black horse was mine now. He was beautiful in my eyes, maybe not so much for someone else looking at him. I had read all the black stallion books, and in my eyes he looked just like that. He actually looked like a fifty-five gallon barrel with legs, a bulldog style quarter horse. I still think he was beautiful.

No one else could ride him, although he never bucked. He would run away with anybody except me, and sometimes he'd run from me. He tolerated me out of friendship, but if he wanted to go one way and I the other; he went his way. No mater how hard you pulled on the reins, his neck was too strong to pull around. When he ran off with someone, he never bucked, but somehow he always came back alone. He would run so fast you couldn't see. Then he would make a very sharp turn. He would finish that turn alone. That wasn't the worst of it. I had seen the lone ranger once too often. I thought Thunder would look great rearing high before we broke into a fast run. I taught him to rear up high, which was impressive I am sure. After he learned that trick, he used it to get people off his back. If they didn't come off with his fast turn, he would rear right over on his back. Nobody ever got crushed, but he was turned into a packhorse after that since that was the only way father could use him. He was my horse, and I rode him, but father was very unhappy with my training. I had ruined him for other people to use. Thunder was never much of a benefit to anyone except me.

Thunder was a very fast horse, and nobody could out run us. I raced him against most of the horses in Palmer. I was never beaten. I did take out a fence or two when he didn't stop. He was about five or six when he came to us, and he was around twenty-two when he went to that big pasture in the sky. I loved him always. I still dream of him. I have had many horses in my life, and I have loved them all. Thunder was that one special horse you meet only once in a lifetime. He was a good friend when I needed one most.

I got to know my older brother, John Joseph, when I was twelve. He was a lot of fun and was so happy to know his brothers and sisters. He took us a lot of places. I went caribou hunting with him up the Glenn Highway. It was very cold that day, close to forty below or better. John Joe drove to where the caribou were crossing the highway. He shot two and both ran over the hill to fall down, about fifty yards from the road but in deep snow. The wind started to blow before we got the first one skinned. I had only worn low shoes for some reason. Stupidity, I think. Well my feet started to freeze up on me, and I had to go back to the truck to get out of the wind. I was no help to my brother at all. The truck had no heater, but my brother had brought his bird dog, Dolly. She was warm, so I just took off my shoes and put my feet on her belly. My feet warmed up, and I was grateful my brother had brought her. John Joe pulled both caribou over to the truck whole. I helped him get them into the back, and we took off for home. By the time we got the thirty miles home, both caribou were frozen solid.

I also went on a hunting trip with John Joe to Southeast Alaska. We traveled by fishing boat. We had a lot of fun on that trip. We fished in the ocean and caught a lot of sharks, which nobody wanted so they had to be cut loose. The captain of the boat pulled up some crab pots, and they had a lot of king crab in them. The king crabs were emptied out in a large fish tote. The fishermen were cracking the crab in half and throwing them into a large pot of boiling water. I grabbed one of those crabs and was going to break it like I saw the men do. That was a bad idea. That crab reached around and grabbed me by the front of my jacket. My arms were too short to keep him off my face. One of the men grabbed the crab off me. That was the end of my help cleaning crabs. I did help eat some a bit later. It seemed fair to me. Afterward, John Joe took me to the beach in the skiff, and we picked up butter clams on the beach. Someone caught some red snapper fish while we were gone. We had a real seafood feast that night, and we didn't have to eat those awful sharks.

I loved my older brother. He had a few bad habits, but I over looked them. Some people in my family did not. John Joe did tell some tall tails, and he had a drinking problem later in life. Also things seemed to stick to his fingers at times, but he was my big brother. The only big brother I ever had, and I thought the sun rose and set in him. John Joe was one that that drew attention with his laughter and wild stories. I do miss John Joe. He was killed in a bad car crash a few years ago. There are still things I would have liked to talk to him about. We really had some fun times together. Life with him around was a wild ride. He always made you laugh, even when you swore you wouldn't. He could really think up some crazy stuff to do. I am so glad he found us, and I got to know him. He taught me a lot about tolerance and brotherly love. He will always be a bright spot in my life.

I got a bit rebellious when I got to be a teenager. I didn't want to take father's hunters out anymore. Those rich men didn't respect us. They treated us like they were our masters, and we were their slaves. I have never responded

Mother with a dead eagle and my sisters

well to that kind of treatment. I was told once that as a native, I didn't know my place. I don't think that man knew his place, as we were a long way from civilization, and he didn't know the way back. I made the rest of his trip miserable. Some of those hunters were used to hunting in Africa and other such places. They wanted me to wash their feet. Well, good luck on that one. My sister, Bonnie, would do it for a tip, but not me. I got good tips when I skinned their trophies for them or helped chase a sheep to them. I would saddle horses, make dinner, or any other thing that was not personal. I just never was that friendly, but we had to help father so he could make the money that we needed to survive. I usually just brought the pack trains into the mountains with supplies or stayed home and looked after the dogs and horses.

I wasn't that easy to get along with there for a while. I could make anyone's trip miserable. I got a few kicks in the butt from father on occasion, which just made me mad. I was very stubborn. After awhile, I figured out how to control my temper and everything went back to normal. I was a mean little girl, but nobody knew what I did to those hunters I didn't like. I would put bad stuff in their food and mice in their sleeping bags. They never knew, and I was happy to keep it to myself. We had a hunter that was a quick draw artist on one hunt. He insisted on wearing his pistol in his sleeping bag. He had to be carried out of the mountains in a helicopter after shooting himself in the foot in his sleeping bag, at least nobody else got shot by him. We also hosted a sharp shooting pair of twin girls from Texas in camp. They could shoot pennies out of the air, but couldn't hit the broad side of the barn from the inside when shooting at game. My sister, Lucy, had to shoot their sheep for them. They paid her to keep quiet though.

Father would stand to one side of hunters and help them get their trophies. When the animal went down father would yell, "You got him! You got him!" Father was an expert shot. I really don't know anyone that could out shoot him. I watched him make incredible shots and always with open sights. He never used a scope. He said it would slow a person down and lose to many animals. I am sure that is true. I have a hard time trying to use a scope, and iron sights never fog up. I would hate to have a grizzly bear too close, and all I had was a gun with a scope.

I think I must have been a lot of trouble for my father when I was thirteen. We seemed to butt heads a lot. I would call him on anything I thought he had done wrong. He really didn't like it. I really should have kept my mouth shut more often, but try and tell a thirteen-year-old anything. He got tired of me after a while and sent me to the convent school. He told me that the nuns and priests would beat me into submission. Well, I was kind of scared to go, but I went anyway. The school was three hundred miles away from my family. I guess father wanted me gone far off. I guess it wasn't just only me he wanted to get rid of. He sent my brother, Johnny, first to California, then a year later to Wyoming to live on the TX Ranch. My sister, Stella, went with Johnny. Another sister went to California to live with my half-sister, Susan, and my little sister, Norma, was sent to live with an uncle in Michigan. Father was finally free. All the children still at home were gone. Mother went to Kansas, and father got a new woman. He got a wife he had divorced forty years before. He stayed with her for pretty much the rest of his life.

Norma did well in Michigan. There were cousins her age. They found she was legally blind and bought her glasses. Come to find out, she wasn't stupid after all. After she could see, she excelled in school. She never went back to Alaska for several years. My sister in California never had it very good. She was scared of the big schools she had to attend. She has always had trouble dealing with people. She was a bit autistic. Going to California just sent her into a tailspin, and she never finished school. She got married early and had a baby. That never worked out for her either, as one of her sisters had to raise her children. She would have done much better to stay in rural Alaska. She never returned to Alaska until after she married. Johnny has the gift of gab and can fit in anywhere. In California, he got on the track team and broke records everywhere in long distance. I think he still holds records there. He had some trouble with street kids. He just wasn't one to take a lot of crap. After that, he went to Wyoming. He had a blast there riding, hunting, and fishing. He really enjoyed all the ranch work. Stella loved Wyoming also.

Me? Well, when I got to the convent I was scared, but it turned out everyone was nice and friendly. There was a lot of food, as much as you wanted to eat. I was used to the law, "He who eats the fastest gets the mostest." At the convent, I learned to slow down a bit when eating. All the nuns and priests were very nice and kind. I found I loved it there at the convent. It changed my attitude and improved me as a person. I guess father got what he wanted for me after all. I loved school and was able to excel in my classes. It was a wonderful school there in Copper Center. The winters are cold, and the summers are warm and filled with mosquitoes, but I loved it. In the winter, the boys got to go on hunting trips and provide meat for the school. The girls helped on the fish wheels in summer. We all helped process meat and fish. Native customs were respected there, although we were expected to act like ladies and gentlemen. Many of my classmates became nuns and priests. I thought I wanted that as well, but decided to return to my family. It would have been just as good a life there as I had somewhere else, just different.

Our dogs hauling logs on the river.

Hilda and Joker, the colt

CHAPTER 13

Things changed as time went by, as is the way of things. Father was finding it hard to get a good hired hand. Young people just were not so interested in the wild life anymore. He placed an advertisement in one of the hunting magazines for help. Boy, did he get a lot of replies! Apparently the lower forty-eight states had a lot of people who didn't fit into society. Father wrote to each of them and weeded out what he was looking for. Mostly he wanted someone who wanted to learn, not someone who already new everything. The know-it-alls are hard to work with. They seem to cause a lot of problems. Father was writing to some friends that had been in some movies with him when he lived in Wyoming as a young man. They wanted to come up for a hunting and fishing trip later that year in the fall.

They were real nice people, and they had a great time with father. Johnny went with them but not me. Father wanted no women in camp. I guess they filled all their game tags, and then they all went fishing for halibut. They brought back quite a lot of fish for mother to can. A bunch of the fish was smoked so they could take it back to California. They had their game meat processed in town and took it back with them along with the heads and hides. Johnny was given an eight by ten glossy photographs autographed with thanks for a great time and best wishes. Johnny still has them today, although at the time, I think he would have preferred to have a bigger tip.

Those were not the only hunters father had that fall. We all had plenty of work to keep us busy. The mountains were our home until late October when the last hunters left, and all the camps were cleaned and readied for winter trapping. All the meat we got from the hunters had to be processed in some way, either canned, dried, smoked, salted, or frozen. We'd often just hang it up in the meat house so the dogs wouldn't get to it. Mother did most of the canning and salting, while father did all the making of jerky and smoking. We had a good store of meat and vegetables that year. The winter wouldn't be so hard. Now we only had to focus on getting wood and feeding livestock. We even got to school most of the year. I loved school, as they had a library, and I loved to read. I read all the books in the library and anything else I could find. I even read all the encyclopedias. Reading was my escape from everything. I would just disappear into a book, and it was hard to get me out. If someone couldn't find me, they would look behind stove or any hidden place, and there I would be with a book. Back to this world I would be forced to come, not happily though.

There were new clothes this year, as we had made our own money to buy what we wanted. We bought new Levis and snap shirts. We got two of each as well as socks and underwear. Johnny and I were able to buy the little girls some clothes too. We all looked good going to school. Well, we thought we did anyway. Father left again for the lower forty-eight to get hunters for the next year so it was just mother and the children. At least we had food this time. Father returned after only a month, as he had trapping to do. Trapping also kept him away from home, but it was necessary to feed and house us all.

Father really loved the wilderness and chose to spend most of his time in the woods trapping, hunting, and fishing. It was the life we all loved and lived. Other people were not what any of us wanted to be around, but we had to for school and making money. I was not that pleasant to be around at anytime. I just didn't like people. I did have friends I liked, but not many though. Some of those friends are still friends today. I still am not a socialite, more of a recluse. But, I'm a lot nicer than I used to be. I still can't stand stupid though.

That next summer I was roaming further from home and meeting more people. Most people weren't that bad I found. Although I still spent a lot of time alone in the hills, I did visit with people that had moved into the hills and valleys near us. A group of people came up and took up homesteads near where we lived. When I say near, I mean within a few miles. The ladies from those families were very nice and always gave us coffee and a snack when we came by. They had a few kids our age. We took them with us to go fishing. We always made sure they got enough fish to make a meal, even if they didn't catch enough themselves. We always caught plenty. Those kids were a lot of fun to go riding with and swimming in the lakes. Most people didn't stay long, as it was a hard life, and these people were no exception. As winter came, the bigger share of them went back to Texas. The rest moved to town. The bush life was not for everyone. They had to work and provide for their families. In winter with road conditions what they were, there would have been no way to hold a job in town. Some of the kids were in our classes in the Palmer school. They often moved away during the winter. We never knew what happened to them. Someone else took up their cabins through the years.

The electric company put in power to our valley as more people lived here now. We got electric lights in our house and barn. Wow! We were like uptown now. We never had a well or inside plumbing, but hey we had lights. The only lights we had were in the front of the house but it made homework easier. Lanterns were still used in the back room. The electricity also gave us a monthly electric bill, which was something we hadn't had before. I am sure it wasn't much, as we only had one light bulb in the house and one in the barn. One in the outhouse would have been nice. We were getting more modern all the time. Father got a radio that worked on electric. We listened to radio shows like The Lone Ranger, The Shadow, and many others. It was great family time together. Sometimes mother would make us snacks to eat while we all sat around the radio. People sent messages to bush folks on the radio show called The Mukluk Telegraph. Mother and father always listened to that show. Sometimes we would hear messages for us; maybe someone was planning on coming up or needed to be called for some reason. It was a good system for delivering messages.

If father needed to call someone, he had to ride a horse or take a dog sled to a lodge ten miles away. The Lodge was the only phone for miles around. If it was summer, father could cut that distance down by riding through the hills instead of following the road, but not in winter, as it was too dangerous. The hills were too steep, which is why the roads were not made along that route. That lodge had a pool table we were allowed to play on, as long as there were no adults that wanted to play. Johnny got quite good at pool. I played well, but not as well as Johnny. He became a little shark. He hustled more than one burger from a tourist, which we would split. If he got two burgers, he took one home for the little girls. They made big burgers at the lodge, without as many vegetables like they have today. The burgers might have some onion and lettuce if we were lucky and sometimes cheese. They sure were good. They weren't better than mother made, but we'd eat them with a bun not sliced bread. Having won the burgers made them taste even better.

It was always fun to ride or just walk somewhere. It didn't matter where. We just enjoyed going. Sometimes we went into town, which was thirty miles away. The ride there was good as we had good, tough horses. Sometimes we rode with people that were going to town for the day. It was fun to be in town for a little while. We would always go see Harry, and we always tried to take him back with us. Most of the time his mother let him go. We were disappointed when he couldn't come along, as we always had plans for some kind of adventure. It was a whole lot of fun when Harry got to go with us though. The thirty-mile ride home was just as fun. It always took us longer to get home with a friend, because we stopped along the way to play in beaver dams and streams. When Harry came back with us, we always had a lunch his mother packed for us. She never let us go home without making something to take for the trail. Of course, we had to stop for to eat that lunch, and it usually led to rock throwing or hill climbing, even trees weren't left unclimbed.

We didn't always go to town together. Sometimes we were invited alone. On one such time, Johnny went with a neighbor's family to church. After they returned home, he stayed pretty late at their house. It was early winter, and there was snow on the ground. He had a five-mile walk to get home in the dark. You could just see the road in the starlight. Well, let him tell you what happened,

> "I was coming home from going to church with the Frizby Family. There was snow, maybe a couple feet, and it was getting dark. When I topped the hill somewhere between there and the mine road, I heard something I believed to be a moose. I looked for a place to hide and spotted a stump that had been pushed over when they were working on the road, or so I thought. I ran to it and jumped on it to try to get behind it. When I did, it stood up. It was a moose

that had been resting in the snow. I could feel her skin moving under my feet. I think I sailed over the snow without touching down until I was back on the road. It didn't take long to get home. I don't even remember much of the run back. Guess I was moving at a pretty good speed."

I am sure that moose was as startled as he was. They probably both ran pretty hard to get out of the area. If there was another moose around, somewhere between all the screaming and brush breaking, it was scared away too. I don't think Johnny even thought about it again.

Johnny grew into quite a good woodsman, which he learned from father. Father was the best woodsman I've ever known. He was a novelty at rich people's parties I am sure. Father was most interested in being in the woods, as he felt the most comfortable there. Really that kind of life took up most of his time. I never felt he had too much use for anything that took him away from his life in the mountains.

When buying supplies for hunting camp, father would buy case lots of fruits and vegetables. For some reason, he always bought a couple case of purple plums. The hunters would eat the peaches, pears and fruit cocktail, but no one ate the purple plums. After hunting season the purple plums were always brought home for mother. I have to give her credit for the numerous ways she found to use those plums. After a few years of eating all those plumbs, the kids took to burying the cans of plums around the camp. That way, we wouldn't have to eat them later in some kind of raisin pie. The canned plums worked well in the winter for bed warmers. You just heat a pot of water to boiling and throw in a can or two of plums. When the cans were boiling hot you threw them into the bottom of your sleeping bag. They stayed warm for a long time and kept your feet warm. Father passed away when he was near one-hundred-years-old, after guiding for over half a century. It left a lot of purple plums buried all over those mountains.

My mother had a hard and difficult life. Mother just was always so tired and could only do so much. She just worked herself to death. Looking back, I think mother was just overwhelmed. She raised us the best she could, keeping us fed and clothed in an adverse environment. Most of us grew up healthy of both body and mind with solid moral values.

We had a childhood that few can even understand in today's world. The joy and freedom of living the life we did far outweighed the hardships we lived. I am grateful for having lived in the time and place where I grew up. It made us strong and self-reliant. People now days can't even relate to such a life, and we have all had the opportunity to bring up our own children to be good woodsman and respectful of nature and culture. I feel knowing how to take care of yourself in the mountains and forests only helps you take responsibility for yourself no matter where you are. I have a wonderful family comprised of many races and cultures.

God has blessed us all.

The Luster Family

If you have enjoyed
Small Moccasin Tracks:
Memories of an Alaskan Mountain Family

Check out Hilda's second memoir:

Johnny and Me:
The Story of Two Alaskan Children Growing Up Wild